The Star-Spangled Banner

The Flag that Inspired the
National Anthem

The Star-Spangled Banner

The Flag that Inspired the National Anthem

Lonn Taylor

National Museum of American History
Smithsonian Institution
in association with
Harry N. Abrams, Inc., Publishers

Francis Scott Key, author of "The Star-Spangled Banner." Portrait attributed to Joseph Wood, about 1825. Walters Art Gallery, Baltimore

Mary Pickersgill, maker of the Star-Spangled Banner. Tinted photograph by P. L. Pickens, about 1850. Pickersgill retirement community, Towson, Md.

Lieutenant Colonel George Armistead, commander of Fort McHenry. Portrait by Rembrandt Peale, commissioned by the Baltimore City Council, 1816. Maryland Historical Society, Baltimore

The
STAR-SPANGLED BANNER
PRESERVATION PROJECT

is made possible by major support from
POLO RALPH LAUREN

Significant leadership and support is provided by
THE PEW CHARITABLE TRUSTS
UNITED STATES CONGRESS
THE JOHN S. AND JAMES L. KNIGHT FOUNDATION

with special thanks to
FIRST LADY HILLARY RODHAM CLINTON
AND THE WHITE HOUSE MILLENNIUM COUNCIL
and
SAVE AMERICA'S TREASURES AT
THE NATIONAL TRUST FOR HISTORIC PRESERVATION
for their leadership

For the Smithsonian Institution:
Editor: Diana Cohen Altman

For Harry N. Abrams, Inc.:
Editor: Nicole Columbus
Designer: Judith Hudson with Barbara Sturman

Library of Congress Cataloging-in-Publication Data
Taylor, Lonn, 1940–
The Star-Spangled Banner : the flag that inspired
the national anthem / Lonn Taylor.
        p.   cm.
Includes bibliographical references and index.
ISBN 0–8109–2940–6 (pbk.)
1. Baltimore, Battle of, 1814. 2. United States—
History—War of 1812—Flags. 3. Flags—United
States—History. 4. Star-Spangled banner (Song).
5. Armistead family. I. Title.

E356.B2 T39 2000
973.5'2—dc21   99–55387

Pages 2 and 3: "A View of the Bombardment of Fort
McHenry," print by J. Bower, Philadelphia, 1816.
National Museum of American History, Smithsonian
Institution, Washington, D.C.

Page 4: The Star-Spangled Banner as exhibited at
the National Museum of American History, 1964–98.
Smithsonian Institution, Washington, D.C.

Page 10: Architect's drawing of the proposed Flag Hall
at the National Museum of History and Technology
(now the National Museum of American History),
about 1960. National Museum of American History,
Smithsonian Institution, Washington, D.C.

Harry N. Abrams, Inc.
100 Fifth Avenue
New York, N.Y. 10011
www.abramsbooks.com

Contents

11 Introduction

15 *Chapter 1:* The Battle of Baltimore

27 *Chapter 2:* The Song

39 *Chapter 3:* The Flag

46 *Chapter 4:* An Armistead Family Treasure

65 *Chapter 5:* The Star-Spangled Banner and
    the Smithsonian Institution

81 *Appendix 1:* "The Star-Spangled Banner,"
    by Francis Scott Key

82 *Appendix 2:* Lt. Col. George Armistead's Official
    Report of the Bombardment of Fort McHenry

85 Notes

89 Bibliography

91 Acknowledgments

Introduction

An American Symbol:
The Star-Spangled Banner

. . . [FRANCIS SCOTT KEY AND JOHN SKINNER] PACED THE
DECK FOR THE RESIDUE OF THE NIGHT IN PAINFUL SUSPENSE.
. . . THEIR GLASSES WERE TURNED TO THE FORT, UNCERTAIN
WHETHER THEY SHOULD SEE THERE THE STARS AND STRIPES,
OR THE FLAG OF THE ENEMY. AT LENGTH THE LIGHT CAME, AND
THEY SAW THAT "OUR FLAG WAS STILL THERE."

—Roger B. Taney to Charles Howard, March 17, 1856

The lyrics to the national anthem of the United States, "The Star-Spangled Banner," hold a deep resonance for many Americans. Phrases such as "the rockets' red glare," and "the bombs bursting in air" have the power to stir patriotic feelings in ways that are immediate and palpable.

Not many people connect the words of the national anthem with the historic event that inspired them, the bombardment of Fort McHenry in Baltimore by a British fleet on September 13–14, 1814, in the midst of the War of 1812. Similarly, few realize that the actual Star-Spangled Banner – the flag that Francis Scott Key anxiously sought on the morning of September 14 – has survived for nearly two centuries. Preserved for scholars to study and for the public to cherish, the original Star-Spangled

Banner has been on display at the Smithsonian Institution in Washington, D.C., since 1907.

The story of the Star-Spangled Banner only begins with Fort McHenry. The enormous, 30-by-42-foot flag has taken on many roles in its long lifetime. When it was made in Baltimore in the summer of 1813, it was a simple garrison flag, one of many such standards that flew over American forts as markers of government property. After the British attacked Baltimore in 1814, the flag gained recognition as the "Star-Spangled Banner" hailed in the popular song by Francis Scott Key. Soon after it became a valued family keepsake for Major George Armistead, the commander of Fort McHenry, offering the Armistead family and their circle of friends a tangible connection to the heroism of the men who fought at Fort McHenry. Baltimoreans occasionally saw the flag displayed on patriotic occasions, courtesy of the Armistead family.

In the emotional atmosphere of the Civil War and its aftermath, Francis Scott Key's song excited a new generation. Americans came to see the flag as a national treasure. Since then Americans have recognized the flag as a primary symbol of the nation's ideals and of the need to preserve those ideals.

Standing in front of the Star-Spangled Banner on a visit to the National Museum of American History in July 1998, President William Jefferson Clinton offered this interpretation of the flag's significance:

> *This Star-Spangled Banner and all its successors have come to embody our country, what we think of as America. It may not be quite the same for every one of us who looks at it, but in the end we all pretty much come out where the framers did. We know we have a country founded on the then revolutionary idea that all of us are created equal, and equally entitled to life, liberty, and the pursuit of happiness. . . . You can neither honor the past, nor imagine the future, without the kind of citizenship*

embodied by all our memories of this flag. So as you see this flag and leave this place, promise yourself that when your great-grandchildren are here, they will not only be able to see the Star-Spangled Banner, it will mean just as much to them as it does to you today.[1]

It is appropriate that the Star-Spangled Banner should have received its baptism by fire during the War of 1812, a turning point in the history of the young republic. Dramatic victories at Baltimore and New Orleans showed the world that a new, untested nation with a new form of government could bring the most powerful monarchy in the world to a standstill. The war ended debates within the republic about the validity of the new form of government. The triumphs freed Americans from the shadow of the mother country and demonstrated that the United States was a nation in its own right.

The war began because Great Britain, engaged in a life-or-death struggle with Napoleon's France, tried to prevent American ships from trading with France. British ships hovered outside of American seaports, stopping American ships, confiscating their cargoes, and impressing American sailors among their crews into British service. Incensed by this interference, the U.S. Congress declared war on June 18, 1812. Western congressmen known as the War Hawks saw the war as an opportunity to seek annexation of British Canada. As soon as war was declared, an American army invaded Canada, but the British quickly repulsed their attack and occupied Detroit. The British continued to devote most of their resources to defeating Napoleon in Europe. British and U.S. military and naval forces clashed along the U.S.–Canadian border, on the Great Lakes, and in actions at sea, but they fought no decisive battles.

Napoleon's abdication in April 1814 freed the British to intensify military actions against the United States. British reinforcements arrived in Canada with the intention of invading New York by way of Lake

Champlain. A second convoy of ships and soldiers went to Bermuda, intending to conduct a series of raids in the Chesapeake Bay region and eventually to seize New Orleans. The British abandoned their advance toward New York when a U.S. naval squadron gained control of Lake Champlain on September 11, 1814, and severed the British supply line. The British raiding force in the Chesapeake, however, managed to land and march to Washington, D.C., which they burned on August 24, 1814.

On September 13–14, American forces repelled British advances on Baltimore. The British forces then sailed for the Gulf of Mexico, where, reinforced by additional troops, they attempted to take New Orleans. On January 8, 1815, General Andrew Jackson and his corps of volunteers defeated the would-be invaders. The Americans ended the war in a blaze of glory. In fact, British and American representatives had already signed a peace treaty in Ghent, Belgium, on December 24, 1814, but word of peace did not reach North America until February 1815.

Although the Ghent treaty addressed none of the issues that caused the war, and no exchanges of territory took place, the War of 1812 severed the United States' remaining ties with the nation's colonial past. The War of 1812 opened the way for Americans to consider the needs of the future and the best means of national development. It turned American eyes away from Europe and toward American resources.

Perhaps most significant, the war instilled in Americans a new sense of national pride – pride that would be expressed in symbols such as the flag and Francis Scott Key's anthem.

1 The Battle of Baltimore

REJOICE, YE PEOPLE OF AMERICA! INHABITANTS OF PHILADELPHIA, NEW YORK, AND BOSTON REJOICE! BALTIMORE HAS NOBLY FOUGHT YOUR BATTLES! THANK GOD, AND THANK THE PEOPLE OF BALTIMORE!

— "A Republican paper of Boston," quoted in
Niles' Weekly Register, October 1, 1814

On August 1, 1814, a convoy of transports carrying 5,000 British troops commanded by Major General Robert Ross and a fleet of warships led by Admiral Sir Alexander Cochrane headed from the British naval station in Bermuda toward Chesapeake Bay.

The British force sought to wreak havoc on the upstart republic's capital at Washington and on the city of Baltimore. The third-largest city in the United States, Baltimore also served as home base for privateers, armed private vessels operating under government license, which had captured or sunk 500 British merchant ships in the two years since the War of 1812 began.

Guided by Rear Admiral George Cockburn, whose ships had been blockading Chesapeake Bay and raiding the small towns on its shores all summer, the British fleet entered Chesapeake Bay on August 16 and made its way up the Patuxent River. While Major General Ross's troops landed at the town of Benedict, Maryland, Admiral Cockburn's boats pursued a flotilla of American gunboats under Commodore Joshua Barney up the river to Pig Point. There, Barney scuttled the gunboats. General Ross's troops marched across the neck of land separating the Patuxent and Potomac Rivers toward Washington. On August 24, at Bladensburg, Maryland, General Ross's troops met and resoundingly defeated a hastily assembled American force twice their size under General William Henry Winder. The Americans broke and ran in the face of the disciplined ranks of British bayonets.

That night the British, led by General Ross and Admiral Cockburn, occupied Washington, where they methodically set fire to the U.S. Capitol, the President's mansion, and other public buildings. A few days later British ships appeared in the Potomac off Alexandria, Virginia. Responding to the pleas of merchants with warehouses full of tobacco and flour, Mayor Charles Simms surrendered. The surrender backfired, and the British confiscated the valuable goods and loaded them onto their ships.

By September 8, Ross, Cockburn, and their respective troops joined Admiral Cochrane and the British fleet at Tangier Island in Chesapeake Bay. The three commanding officers planned their strategy for capturing Baltimore.

The plan called for a combined land and sea operation, beginning with a landing by Ross's troops at North Point, Maryland, at the mouth of the Patapsco River. Ross's troops were to march thirteen miles northwestward up Long Log Lane and the Philadelphia Road to the city of

OPPOSITE: *The Battle of Baltimore, September 12–14, 1814. Fort McHenry National Monument and Historic Shrine, Baltimore, Md.*

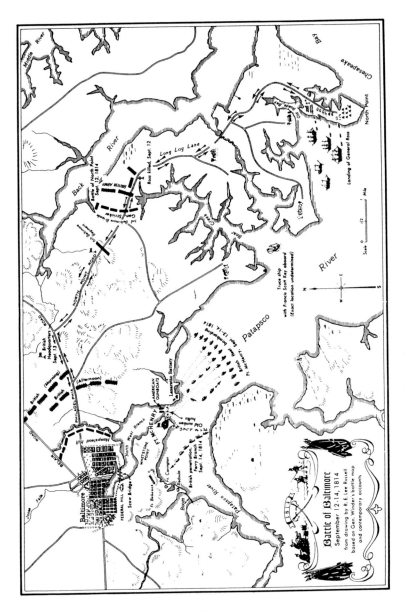

Battle of Baltimore
September 12-14, 1814
from drawing by R. E. Lee Russell
based on Gen. Winder's battle map
and contemporary accounts

Baltimore. Meanwhile, Cochrane's ships would bombard Fort McHenry in order to enter Baltimore's inner harbor and support Ross's troops as they pressed their attack on the city.

In the days following the British burning of Washington, American Major General Samuel Smith, the commander of the city's defenses, heavily fortified the eastern approaches to Baltimore in anticipation of an attack from that direction. Nearly 15,000 militiamen and 100 pieces of artillery lined a half mile of trenches and earthworks along both sides of the Philadelphia Road along the crest of Hampstead Hill. More troops served as a forward line thrown across the narrow peninsula and up the Patapsco from the peninsula that ended in North Point.

Smith paid particular attention to protecting Fort McHenry, which was about eight miles up the Patapsco from North Point and which guarded Baltimore Harbor. A floating boom made of chained-together ship masts blocked the mouth of the harbor. Just beyond, a row of sunken hulks served as further deterrent. The fort itself was armed with fifty-seven 18-, 24-, and 36-pound naval guns and artillery pieces with a range of one and a half miles. Both inside the fort and in the earthworks around it, a 250-man artillery garrison, supplemented by nearly 750 battle-ready infantry regulars, sailors, and militiamen, prepared for battle.

Commanding the U.S. troops at Fort McHenry was Major George Armistead, a professional regular army soldier who in 1813 had distinguished himself at the capture of Fort George on the Canadian frontier.

From the beginning, the British did not anticipate the Americans' strong defense. Early in the morning of September 12, Ross's troops landed at North Point. Just after noon they encountered the American forward line. In the ensuing battle, an American sharpshooter killed General Ross, who had been riding back from the front of his line to call up reinforcements. The Americans withstood British fire for nearly an hour before withdrawing toward their main line.

The British spent a miserable, rainy night encamped on the battle-ground. Early the next morning, September 13, Lieutenant Colonel Arthur Brooke, who had assumed Ross's command, led his men forward to within sight of the American main line. Brooke immediately realized that he could not defeat the Americans by a daytime frontal attack. He spent the day maneuvering his troops in the rain and probing the American defenses for a possible night attack.[1]

The Flag's Baptism by Fire

By mid-afternoon on September 12, three frigates, *Seahorse*, *Surprise*, and *Severn*, had anchored in the Patapsco about five miles from the fort. The bomb vessels *Meteor*, *Devastation*, *Aetna*, *Volcano*, and *Terror*, accompanied by the rocket ship *Erebus*, had approached to within two and a half miles, safely out of reach of the fort's guns.

The British maritime arsenal's most formidable weapons, the bomb vessels were specially constructed shallow-draft ships that carried 10- and 13-inch mortars with ranges of two miles. The mortars fired huge spherical bombshells filled with powder that exploded over the target, scattering deadly shards of shrapnel. *Erebus* was armed with Congreve rockets, which carried large amounts of incendiary and explosive materials in their warheads. Fired in salvos, the rockets made a terrifying whooshing noise as they passed overhead and ignited fires wherever they landed.

The British started bombarding the fort at 6:30 in the morning on September 13 and continued throughout the day and the following night. At first the fort returned the fire, but the British ships soon pulled back out of range of the fort's guns while continuing to fire their own. At 10:00 in the morning Major Armistead ordered his gunners to cease firing. For the next few hours Armistead's men crouched in trenches and behind walls while the bombs burst around them. "We were like pigeons tied by the legs to be shot at," recalled Judge Joseph H. Nicholson, a commanding officer of the Artillery Fencibles, in a letter to Secretary of War James Monroe, September 21, 1814.

At about 3:00 in the afternoon on the 13th, the British bomb ships moved in for the kill, returning to within range of the fort's guns. The American gunners responded with fire that so badly damaged *Erebus* that she had to be towed back out of range. Also hit, *Devastation* and *Volcano* retreated to their previous positions and maintained their bombardment from a safe distance. The bombs continued to fall at the rate of nearly one a minute for the rest of the afternoon and into the night. The men in the fort watched the explosions light up the sky like lightning flashes. Baltimoreans could clearly see the stream of sparks from the bombs' fuses arching through the air. The sounds of a torrential rain, which had worsened during the day, mixed with peals of thunder, which in turn joined the cacophony caused by the mortars, bombs, and rockets.

During the night of the 13th, the British strategy began to unravel. About midnight Admiral Cochrane decided that he had no chance of getting his ships past Fort McHenry and the line of sunken ships that blocked the entrance to the harbor. He sent Lieutenant Colonel Brooke a message to that effect. At about the same time, an elite group of 1,200 British marines and seamen led by Captain Charles Napier set out from Cochrane's ships to create a diversion that would aid Brooke's night attack even if the larger ships could not get into the harbor. Napier's men set out in the dark in a single file of barges with muffled oars, aiming to disembark behind the fort in the Ferry Branch of the Patapsco. In the darkness and rain, however, the last nine boats in the line got lost and headed instead toward the inner harbor. The other boats were discovered by the alert artillerymen at Battery Babcock and Fort Covington, two of the batteries outside the fort.

After a fierce artillery duel, the British barges retreated to their mother ships. Brooke reluctantly gave up any idea of attack and began to withdraw his troops back to their landing place at North Point. About 2:00 in the morning, the bomb vessels resumed their fire, which had been suspended until Napier's boats were safely back. By 4:00 the British slowed the bombing, and by about 7:00 they stopped firing. Within two hours the defenders of the fort saw the bomb vessels and frigates move down the river to join the main fleet at North Point, where Brooke's men were about to start their embarkation. Just over 24 hours after launching their first bomb, the British had given up their attempt. Baltimore was saved.

"As the last vessel spread her canvas to the wind," wrote British midshipman Robert Barrett, who had witnessed the bombardment from the frigate *Hebrus*, "the Americans hoisted a splendid and superb ensign on their battery, and at the same time fired a gun of defiance." American Private Isaac Munroe, of the Baltimore Fencibles, saw the same flag and recorded it in a letter he wrote to a friend in Boston on September 17. "At dawn on the 14th," he said, "our morning gun was fired, the flag hoisted, Yankee Doodle played, and we all appeared in full view of a formidable and mortified enemy, who calculated upon our surrender in 20 minutes after the commencement of the action." The flag that both men saw was the flag now known as the Star-Spangled Banner.[2]

George Armistead and the "Old Defenders" Honored

By September 16, 1814, the last British ship had left the harbor; the sky over Fort McHenry was still, except for the sounds of victory echoing from the city. Celebrations erupted up and down the East Coast, and Baltimoreans rejoiced that the city had been spared Washington's fate. Major George Armistead and his men, along with Major General Samuel Smith and his soldiers on Hampstead Hill, were instant heroes. Armistead took pride in the fact that his losses amounted to only four men killed and 24 wounded. According to his estimate, 1,500 to 1,800 bombs had been fired at the fort, 400 of which fell within its walls.

Baltimoreans took particular pleasure that the victory came just weeks after the cowardly Washingtonians had run away, leaving the British to burn their city. In their eyes, a group of local citizens had defeated the greatest army and navy in the world. The veterans of North Point and Fort McHenry became known as the Old Defenders, and they marched in parades in Baltimore on September 12 for the rest of their lives. Celebrations on that day, known as Defenders' Day, have endured as a Baltimore tradition.

Although George Armistead became a hero in Maryland, he started life as a Virginian, born on his mother's Baylor family plantation, Newmarket, in Caroline County, on April 10, 1780. He was related to patrician Virginia families on both sides, but he also had important Baltimore ties. On October 26, 1810, during a previous tour of duty at Fort McHenry, he had married Louisa Hughes, the daughter of Christopher Hughes, a wealthy Baltimore silversmith and brickyard owner. Louisa's brother, Christopher Hughes, Jr., was married to Sophia Smith, the daughter of Major General Samuel Smith, who was not only a hero of the Revolution but also a wealthy Baltimore merchant and a longstanding member of Congress.[3]

Within days of the battle, President James Madison promoted Armistead to the rank of brevet lieutenant colonel, citing his "gallant conduct . . . during the late attack and bombardment." The following September, on the first anniversary of the battle at North Point, the city of Baltimore invited Armistead, along with Major General Smith and General John Stricker, who had commanded the forward line at North Point, to lay the cornerstone for the Battle Monument in downtown Baltimore. A memorial to those who died at North Point

13-inch British bombshell of the type fired at Fort McHenry. National Museum of American History, Smithsonian Institution, Washington, D.C.

and Fort McHenry, the Battle Monument still stands in the heart of Baltimore.

In 1816 the Baltimore City Council commissioned Rembrandt Peale to paint Armistead's portrait to hang in the City Council Chamber. A group of citizens presented Lieutenant Colonel Armistead with what the *Niles' Weekly Register* described as "a superb piece of plate, resembling a bomb-shell, to serve as a great bowl by lifting the cover, with appropriate supporters, descriptions, and devices." The silver service consists of an oval tray, a silver bowl with a cover supported by four silver eagles on a round base, a ladle, and ten silver cups. The bowl was made by Philadelphia silversmiths Thomas Fletcher and Sidney Gardiner, and the ladle and cups are marked by Andrew E. Warner of Baltimore. A view of Fort McHenry is engraved on one side, and an inscription appears on the other, as follows:

Presented by a number of citizens of Baltimore to Lt. Col. George Armistead for his gallant and successful defense of Fort McHenry during the bombardment by a large British force on the 12th and 13th of September when upwards of 1500 shells were thrown; 400 of which fell within the area of the Fort and some of them of the diameter of this vase.

Lieutenant Colonel Armistead continued to be honored after his untimely death on April 25, 1818, at the age of thirty-nine. The cause of his death is not known. His funeral procession, which featured a number of military bands stationed along the route, was the largest Baltimoreans

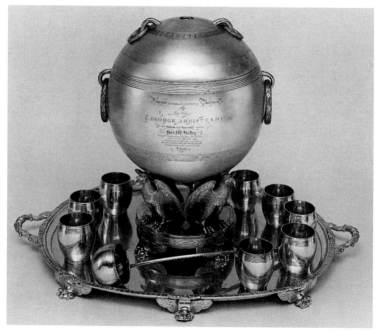

Bombshell-shaped silver punchbowl, cups, ladle, and tray presented to Lieutenant Colonel Armistead by the citizens of Baltimore, 1816. National Museum of American History, Smithsonian Institution, Washington, D.C.

had ever seen. Guns fired at one-minute intervals by an artillery battery on Federal Hill punctuated the ceremonies.

In 1827 the City of Baltimore erected a monument to Armistead at the City Spring on Saratoga Street. A marble tablet flanked by two marble cannons and surmounted by a flaming bomb, the monument later fell into disrepair. In 1861 it was dismantled and its remnants placed in storage. In 1882 the marble cannons and flaming bomb were incorporated into a second monument to Armistead on Eutaw Place. This structure was later moved to Federal Hill, where it stands today, overlooking the very harbor Armistead defended. In 1914, as part of Baltimore's Star-Spangled Banner Centennial celebration, a third monument to Armistead, a bronze statue by Edward Berge, was erected on the grounds of Fort McHenry.[4]

DEFENCE OF FORT M^cHENRY.

The annexed song was composed under the following circumstances—
A gentleman had left Baltimore, in a flag of truce for the purpose of getting released from the British fleet, a friend of his who had been captured
at Marlborough.—He went as far as the mouth of the Patuxent, and was
not permitted to return lest the intended attack on Baltimore should be
disclosed. He was therefore brought up the Bay to the mouth of the Patapsco, where the flag vessel was kept under the guns of a frigate, and
he was compelled to witness the bombardment of Fort M'Henry, which
the Admiral had boasted that he would carry in a few hours, and
that the city must fall. He watched the flag at the Fort through the
whole day with an anxiety that can be better felt than described, until
the night prevented him from seeing it. In the night he watched the Bomb
Shells, and at early dawn his eye was again greeted by the proudly waving
flag of his country.

Tune—Anacreon in Heaven.

O ! say can you see by the dawn's early light,
    What so proudly we hailed at the twilight's last gleaming,
Whose broad stripes and bright stars through the perilous fight,
    O'er the ramparts we watch'd, were so gallantly streaming?
And the Rockets' red glare, the Bombs bursting in air,
Gave proof through the night that our Flag was still there;
      O ! say does that star-spangled Banner yet wave,
      O'er the Land of the free, and the home of the brave?

On the shore dimly seen through the mists of the deep,
    Where the foe's haughty host in dread silence reposes,
What is that which the breeze, o'er the towering steep,
    As it fitfully blows, half conceals, half discloses ?
Now it catches the gleam of the morning's first beam,
In full glory reflected new shines in the stream,
      'Tis the star spangled banner, O ! long may it wave
      O'er the lard of the free and the home of the brave

And where is that band who so vauntingly swore
    That the havoc of war and the battle's confusion,
A home and a country, shall leave us no more ?
    Their blood has washed out their foul footsteps pollution
No refuge could save the hireling and slave,
From the terror of flight or the gloom of the grave,
      And the star-spangled banner in triumph doth wave,
      O'er the Land of the Free, and the Home of the Brave

O! thus be it ever when freemen shall stand,
    Between their lov'd home, and the war's desolation,
Blest with vict'ry and peace, may the Heav'n rescued land,
    Praise the Power that hath made and preserv'd us a nation !
Then conquer we must, when our cause it is just,
And this be our motto—" In God is our Trust ;"
      And the star-spangled Banner in triumph shall wave,
      O'er the Land of the Free, and the Home of the Brave.

*The first printing of "Defence of Fort McHenry," which later became
"The Star-Spangled Banner," 1814. Maryland Historical Society, Baltimore*

2 The Song

SO LONG AS PATRIOTISM DWELLS AMONG US, SO LONG WILL THIS SONG BE THE THEME OF OUR NATION.

— *Baltimore American,* January 13, 1843

Of all the tributes paid to the American heroes of Fort McHenry, the most enduring is the victory song that became our national anthem.

A 35-year-old District of Columbia lawyer and amateur poet, Francis Scott Key was more than a bystander during the September 13–14 bombardment of Fort McHenry. He had accompanied John S. Skinner, a civilian employee of the Department of State and of the Commissary General for Prisoners, aboard one of the British ships to seek the release of an American civilian, Dr. William Beanes of Upper Marlboro, Maryland, who was being held prisoner. The British commanders Admiral Cochrane and General Ross agreed to release Dr. Beanes, but they stipulated that all three Americans remain with the British fleet until the end of the attack on Baltimore.

Key and Skinner nervously paced the deck of their vessel all through the night, listening to the noise of the bombardment and straining to see through the smoke and rain if the flag was still flying over Fort McHenry.

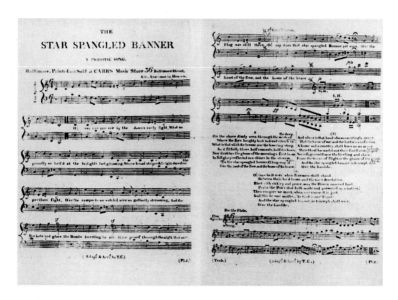

The first sheet-music issue of "The Star-Spangled Banner," printed by Thomas Carr's music store, Baltimore, 1814. Maryland Historical Society, Baltimore

When morning came on the 14th, they could see the fort's garrison flag proudly flying over the battlements. Key exultantly started jotting down the beginnings of a poem on the back of a letter that was in his pocket.

Francis Scott Key initially published his hastily scribbled impressions of the Fort McHenry victory as a poem. This first printing, distributed as a broadside, included a note that the song should be sung to the British melody "The Anacreontic Song," popularly known as "Anacreon in Heaven." Not long after, Thomas Carr's music store published words and music together in the form of sheet music, under the title "The Star-Spangled Banner." The song gained slowly but steadily in popularity in the years before the Civil War. By 1861 it shared with "Yankee Doodle" and "Hail Columbia" the distinction of being played and sung on most patriotic occasions. Nonetheless, the song did not become the congressionally recognized national anthem until 1931.

When Francis Scott Key died on January 11, 1843, flags in Washington and Baltimore were lowered to half-mast, and the U.S. Supreme Court adjourned for one day in his memory. Key had never written a detailed account of the circumstances that surrounded his writing of the poem. After his death, John S. Skinner and Roger B. Taney, who was Chief Justice of the U.S. Supreme Court and Key's brother-in-law, each published accounts of those events. Skinner published an account in the *Baltimore Patriot and Gazette* on May 19, 1849. Taney wrote a letter to Charles Howard on March 17, 1856, that described at length a conversation he had with Key several weeks after the bombardment. In 1857 Robert Carter and Brothers published Taney's letter as an introduction to Henry V. D. Jones's *Poems of the Late Francis S. Key, Esq.* From these narratives historians have pieced together the story of how Key came to write "The Star-Spangled Banner."

Francis Scott Key: Eyewitness to History

Although most Americans know that Francis Scott Key wrote the national anthem, many do not know how a mild-mannered, deeply religious attorney came to be in the midst of one of the most dramatic battles in American history.

Francis Scott Key's mission to the British fleet stemmed from an incident that occurred in the aftermath of the British burning of Washington. While the British retraced their steps to their landing place at Benedict, Maryland, and reembarked on their transports, a hundred or so stragglers remained behind, robbing farms along the roads between Washington and Benedict. On August 27 Dr. William Beanes, a leading citizen of Upper Marlboro whose house had served as Major General Ross's headquarters for a night on the British army's march toward

Washington, organized a posse to stop the pillagers. Beanes and his companions rounded up several of the British marauders and locked them in the local jail. One of the soldiers escaped, and the next day a group of British cavalrymen arrested Beanes and his companions and took them to the British fleet as hostages.

When the Americans released their prisoners, the British freed all of their hostages, except for Beanes. Major General Ross locked Beanes in the brig of Admiral Cochrane's flagship, *Tonnant*. Beanes's friends and neighbors immediately set out to obtain his release. One such friend, Richard West, traveled to Georgetown to see Key, who was his wife's brother-in-law, and asked him to negotiate for Beanes's freedom. On September 1 Key agreed to do what he could and went to see President Madison, who referred him to General John Mason, the U.S. Commissary for Prisoners.

On September 2 General Mason approved Key's mission and gave him a letter addressed to Ross, setting forth the government's case for Beanes's release as a civilian noncombatant. Mason instructed Key to go to Baltimore and contact John S. Skinner, the U.S. government's agent for dealing with the British forces in the Chesapeake, who would take Key to the British fleet. Skinner had been the main means of communication between the government and the British blockading fleet in the Chesapeake for more than a year, and he was well known to Admiral Cockburn and his officers.

Key left for Baltimore on September 3, carrying with him Mason's letter to Ross as well as a bundle of letters from British soldiers who were prisoners in Washington. Some of the letters praised the Americans for giving medical assistance to wounded British troops.

Key arrived in Baltimore on the 4th, and on the 5th he and Skinner set out in a 60-foot, flag-of-truce sloop, probably the *President*.[1] Skinner and Key found the British fleet down the Chesapeake, near the mouth of the Potomac, and were welcomed aboard Admiral Cochrane's flagship, *Tonnant.* That night they dined with General Ross and Admiral Cochrane and discussed Beanes's status. At some point in the evening, Ross was persuaded to release his prisoner.

Taney's and Skinner's accounts agree that Key, Skinner, and Beanes were then told that, as witnesses to preparations for the attack, including conversations between Ross and Cochrane, they would have to remain with the British fleet until after the attack on Baltimore. Cochrane arranged their transfer to the frigate *Surprise,* which then took their sloop in tow.

On Saturday, September 10, Cochrane agreed to return the Americans to their own sloop, along with a guard of British marines. On the 11th the fleet arrived at the mouth of the Patapsco River, and the flag-of-truce sloop was anchored somewhere in Old Roads Bay, northwest of North Point. It was from this vantage point that Key, Skinner, and Beanes heard the battle at North Point on the 12th and watched the bombardment on the 13th and 14th.

According to Taney, Key started composing his famous poem as he watched the enemy bomb vessels pulling back toward the fleet and observed the flag streaming over the fort and did not finish the poem until minutes before reaching shore on the 16th. Taney indicated that Key began with "brief notes . . . upon the back of a letter which he happened to have in his pocket."[2]

Key copied the four verses of the poem and on September 17 showed a copy to his wife's sister's husband, Judge Joseph H. Nicholson, chief justice of the Baltimore courts, asking Nicholson what he thought of it. Judge Nicholson, who had commanded a volunteer company in the fort during the bombardment, reacted enthusiastically. Either he or Skinner — the accounts differ — took the poem to the office of the *Baltimore American,* where it was set in type and printed as a broadside.

The earliest known manuscript of "The Star-Spangled Banner," probably written on September 15, 1814, in Francis Scott Key's hand. Key is believed to have given this manuscript to his wife's brother-in-law, Judge Joseph H. Nicholson, who encouraged Key to publish his poem. Maryland Historical Society, Baltimore

Entitled "Defence of Fort McHenry," the broadside featured a short introductory paragraph, likely written by Judge Nicholson, that described the circumstances under which the lyrics were composed. It also contained the instruction that the words be sung to the tune "Anacreon in Heaven." The broadsides were taken to Fort McHenry, where every man received a copy.

Judge Nicholson evidently kept one of Key's manuscript copies. That manuscript, which was passed on to Nicholson's granddaughter Rebecca Lloyd Shippen, is today in the collection of the Maryland Historical Society.

On September 20 the text was published in the Baltimore *Patriot*, and on September 21 in the *Baltimore American*. By mid-October it had been printed in at least seventeen other papers in cities along the East Coast. Sometime before November 18, Thomas Carr's music store in Baltimore published "The Star-Spangled Banner" in sheet-music form.

More than ninety years after the song was written, Oscar Sonneck, Chief of the Division of Music at the Library of Congress, undertook a scholarly investigation of its history in which he attempted to reconcile Taney's and Skinner's accounts with other pieces of evidence about the song. The Library of Congress first published his *Report on "The Star-Spangled Banner," "Hail Columbia," "America," and "Yankee Doodle"* in 1909. Revised in 1914, the book remains one of the standard works on the subject. In 1969 Edward G. Howard and P. W. Filby of the Maryland Historical Society, in the course of producing an exhibition about "The Star-Spangled Banner," reexamined Skinner's and Taney's accounts in the light of additional evidence that had emerged since Sonneck's work was published. Howard and Filby's conclusions were published in the exhibition's catalogue, *Star-Spangled Books,* published by the Maryland Historical Society in 1972. These twentieth-century scholars have enabled modern historians to construct a fairly accurate chronology of the events that led to the writing and publication of Key's poem.

From Popular Tune to National Anthem

"Anacreon in Heaven," the popular British tune Francis Scott Key chose to accompany his inspirational lyrics, was widely known in America during the early nineteenth century. Historians believe that Key probably had the melody in mind as he was composing the poem.

At least a half dozen American songbooks published before 1814, among them the two-volume *Baltimore Musical Miscellany* (1804 and 1805), included the tune. In 1805 Key himself had used the melody for a poem he wrote in honor of Stephen Decatur, entitled "When the Warrior Returns from the Battle Afar."[3] That song, like "The Star-Spangled Banner," has four verses. It begins:

> *When the warrior returns from the battle afar*
> *To the home and the country he has nobly defended*
> *Oh, warm be the welcome to gladden his ear*
> *And loud be the joys that his perils are ended!*
> *In the full tide of song, let his fame roll along*
> *To the feast flowing board let us gratefully throng*
> *Where mixed with the olive the laurel shall wave*
> *And form a bright wreath for the brow of the brave.*

The last two lines appear in each of the four verses. The third verse contains the couplet, "And pale beamed the Crescent, its splendor obscured / By the star-spangled flag of our nation." The poem appears second in Henry V. D. Jones's 1857 edition of Key's poems, just after "The Star-Spangled Banner."

"Anacreon in Heaven" is often misleadingly described as an old English drinking song. Its foreign, seemingly disreputable origin was in the 1920s advanced as an argument against congressional recognition of "The Star-Spangled Banner" as a national anthem. "Drinking song," in the sense of students with linked arms and raised steins, is in fact a misnomer.

Actually the tune was written in 1775 or 1776 by John Stafford Smith, a London composer of secular and sacred music, to accompany words written by Ralph Tomlinson. It was the "constitutional song" of a mid- to late eighteenth-century gentlemen's musical club called the Anacreontic Society, after the sixth-century B.C.E. Greek poet Anacreon, who wrote a number of short verses in praise of wine and women.

About a dozen times a year, Anacreontic Society members assembled in rooms above various London taverns to play instrumental music and dine together. Guests at the concerts included composers George Frederick Haydn and Johann Nepomuk Hummel, and the meetings were described in 1787 as being "conducted under the strictest influence of propriety and decorum." After a concert lasting two or so hours, the members would adjourn for a cold supper, followed by lighthearted songs performed by the members. The meeting continued with the singing of "Anacreon in Heaven," usually performed as a solo by the club's president. The words of the song invoked the spirit of the Greek poet to inspire the club's members:

> *To Anacreon in Heaven, where he sat in full glee,*
> *A few sons of harmony sent a petition*
> *That he their inspirer and patron would be;*
> *When this answer arrived from the jolly old Grecian.*
> *"Voice fiddle and flute, no longer be mute,*
> *I'll lend you my name, and inspire you to boot,*
> *And besides I'll instruct you like me to entwine*
> *The myrtle of Venus with Bacchus's vine."*

The song continued in the inspirational vein for three more verses.

No one has seriously doubted that Ralph Tomlinson penned the words, but late-nineteenth- and early-twentieth-century scholars debated who wrote the tune. Some advanced the names of Samuel Arnold, the last president of the Anacreontic Society, whereas others credited Turlough O'Carolan, an Irish composer who died in 1738. Still others contended that the song had its origins in an Irish tune called "Royal Inniskilling." In his 1909 *Report on "The Star-Spangled Banner,"* Oscar Sonneck was able to prove John Stafford Smith's authorship to most scholars' satisfaction. "The Star-Spangled Banner" is catalogued under the name of John Stafford Smith in libraries to this day.[4]

The slow but steady growth in popularity of "The Star-Spangled Banner" in the years before the Civil War can be traced by its appearance in popular songbooks of the period. It is included in songbooks published in 1817, 1818, 1820, and 1831. It also was the first song one saw upon opening *The Select Warbler* (1834), *The Singer's Own Book* (1835), *The United States Songster* (1836), as well as *The American Songster* (1845). Eighteen sheet-music editions are known to have been published between 1814 and 1851. Perhaps a more telling indication of the song's growing popularity is the wealth of mid-century songs set to its tune, which by now was cited as "The Star-Spangled Banner." A Whig party songbook published in 1840, *The Harrison Medal Minstrel,* contained no fewer than eight songs extolling the virtues of Presidential candidate William Henry Harrison to be sung to the tune of "The Star-Spangled Banner." Campaign songbooks in every subsequent presidential campaign until the Civil War included songs set to the tune.

By the 1840s, "The Star-Spangled Banner" was popular enough to make its tune an attractive vehicle for parody. In 1843 the *Cold Water Magazine* published a temperance parody that began, "Oh! Who has not seen, by the dawn's early light / Some poor bloated drunkard to his home weakly reeling / With blear eyes and red nose most revolting to sight / Yet still in his breast not a throb of shame feeling?"[5]

In addition to Sonneck, George J. Svejda, who wrote a detailed history of "The Star-Spangled Banner" for the National Park Service in 1969, concluded that the song's popularity increased enormously during the Civil War. Because the song extolled the national flag, which was a symbol of loyalty to the Union, Northerners enthusiastically embraced it as a patriotic song in the North. It was performed at public appearances of President and Mrs. Abraham Lincoln. It was played by countless military bands and sung, both as a solo and in chorus, on hundreds of other occasions in the North. It was the music to which Union armies entered New Orleans, Savannah, Richmond, and many other Southern towns. Hundreds of thousands of Union veterans associated the tune with the excitement and emotion of their war experiences.

American popular sentiment doubtless contributed to the song's progress toward the status of national anthem in the 1890s and the early 1900s. The first official step in that direction was taken in 1889 by the Secretary of the Navy, who issued orders requiring that "The Star-Spangled Banner" be played by all Navy bands at morning colors, the ceremony at which the flag was raised each day. The next year the Secretary of the Navy ordered the U.S. Marine Band to play it at the close of their public performances. The band's annual national tours, initiated in 1891, did much to reinforce the song's popularity. In 1895 Army regulations made the tune the prescribed music to be played as the flag was lowered at evening colors, and in 1904 the Navy amended its regulations to include both morning and evening colors. In 1903 the Navy issued General Order No. 139, which required all officers and men to stand at attention while "The Star-Spangled Banner" was played. The Army issued a similar regulation in 1904. In 1917 both the Army and the

Navy designated "The Star-Spangled Banner" as "the national anthem of the United States" for ceremonial purposes.[6]

Congressional recognition of the song as a national anthem, however, did not come until 1931. Although the Daughters of the American Revolution discussed petitioning Congress to make such a designation as early as 1897, the first bill to do so was not introduced until 1912, by Congressman George Edmond Foss of Illinois. It failed to reach the floor of the House, as did fifteen subsequent bills and resolutions introduced between 1912 and 1917. As Congressman George Murray Hulbert told Alfred J. Carr, the president of the Maryland Society of the War of 1812, there was simply not enough public interest in the matter to goad Congress into action.

In 1918 Mrs. Reuben Ross Holloway, president of the Maryland State Society, United States Daughters of 1812, joined forces with Congressman J. Charles Linthicum of Baltimore to press for congressional recognition of the song as the national anthem. A series of bills introduced by Linthicum between 1918 and 1927 died in committee. But in 1929 Holloway succeeded in gaining support for the next Linthicum bill from various patriotic organizations. The bill making "The Star-Spangled Banner" the national anthem of the United States passed both the House and the Senate and was signed into law by President Herbert Hoover on March 3, 1931.[7]

3 The Flag

A SUPERB AND SPLENDID ENSIGN . . .

— Robert Barrett, British midshipman and eyewitness to British bombardment of Fort McHenry, describing the Star-Spangled Banner, *United Service Journal*, 1841

The flag that so impressed and inspired Francis Scott Key on the morning of September 14, 1814, was made for Fort McHenry under a government contract by a Baltimore flagmaker, Mary Pickersgill, in the summer of 1813. When Major George Armistead arrived in Baltimore to take command of the fort that June, he informed Major General Samuel Smith, "We, Sir, are ready at Fort McHenry to defend Baltimore against invading by the enemy. . . . Except that we have no suitable ensign to display over the Star Fort [Fort McHenry], and it is my desire to have a flag so large that the British will have no difficulty in seeing it from a distance."

At about that same time someone, probably James Calhoun, the U.S. Army's Deputy Commissary Officer in Baltimore, ordered two flags from Mary Pickersgill: a garrison flag, 30 by 42 feet, and a smaller storm flag, 17 by 25 feet. Although it seems large today, the garrison flag was a standard size for the time, about one-fourth the size of a modern basketball court. Garrison flags were intended to fly over forts on flag-poles as high as ninety feet and to be seen from great distances. Armistead seems to have had a special fondness for large flags: when he was stationed at Fort Niagara in 1802 he had requested a flag 36 feet wide and 48 feet long.[1]

The Fort McHenry flags were delivered to the fort on August 19, 1813. On October 27 Mrs. Pickersgill received $405.90 for the large flag and $168.54 for the smaller one. The receipt for payment, endorsed on the reverse by Major Armistead and signed for by Mary Pickersgill's niece, Eliza Young, is in the collection of the Star-Spangled Banner Flag House and 1812 Museum, the site of Mary Pickersgill's former home in Baltimore.

Born in Philadelphia on February 12, 1776, Mary Young Pickersgill was an experienced flagmaker who learned the art from her mother, Rebecca Young. Mary's father, William Young, died when she was two years old, and Rebecca supported herself and her children by making blankets, uniforms, and flags for George Washington's Continental Army. On October 2, 1795, Mary married John Pickersgill, a Baltimore merchant. The couple lived in Philadelphia until John Pickersgill's death in 1805, after which Mary and her daughter, Caroline, along with Mary's mother, Rebecca, moved to Baltimore.[2]

The garrison flag that Mary Pickersgill made for Fort McHenry is now at the National Museum of American History. The red and white stripes and the blue union in the corner were made from English woolen bunting dyed blue with indigo and red with tin-mordanted cochineal and madder. The stars are cotton and are sewn into the union by reverse appliqué method, in which each star was sewn into place on one side of the flag and the cloth on the other side was then cut away to reveal it. Each star is about two feet across, and each stripe is about 23 inches wide. Since the bunting came in 18-inch widths, a complete width and a partial width were sewn together to produce each stripe. The hoist, the part of the flag closest to the pole, was probably folded over to reinforce the seam area, and a separate sleeve, probably of linen, was sewn to it. A length of rope with leather loops on each end could be passed through the linen sleeve. Both the sleeve and the rope are now missing from the flag.[3]

In making the flag, Mary Pickersgill was helped by her 13-year-old daughter, Caroline, and probably also by her mother, as well as by her nieces Eliza and Margaret Young. More than sixty years later, Caroline Pickersgill Purdy wrote to George Armistead's daughter, Georgiana Armistead Appleton, who was planning to lend the Star-Spangled Banner to the 1876 Philadelphia Centennial Exhibition. Purdy recalled the hours that she and her mother had spent making the enormous flag:

> *Mrs. Appleton.*
>
> *Dear Madam,*
>
> *. . . I take the liberty to send you a few particulars about the "Flag."*
> *It was made by my mother Mrs. Mary Pickersgill, and I assisted her. . . .*
> *My mother was selected by Commo. Berney and General Stricker (family connections) to make the "Star-Spangled Banner," which she did, being an exceedingly patriotic woman. The flag being so very large, my mother was obliged to obtain permission from the proprietors of Claggetts brewery which was in our neighborhood to spread it out in their malt house; and I remember seeing my mother down on the floor, placing the stars: after the completion of the flag, she superintended the topping of it, having it fastened in the most secure manner to prevent its being torn away by balls; the wisdom of her precaution was shown during the engagement; many shots piercing it, but it still remained firm to the staff. Your father declared that no one but the maker of the flag should mend it, and requested that the rents be merely bound round. The flag contained, I*

*think, four hundred yards of bunting, and my mother worked many
nights until 12 o'clock to complete it in the given time.*

Caroline Pickersgill Purdy ended her letter to Georgiana Armistead
Appleton on a sad note, saying,

*I am widowed and childless, and now find myself, in my seventy-sixth
year, in feeble health and with the barest pittance of support. My friends
here in Balto. have suggested that if these particulars meet with your
approbation, and were placed on a card attached to the flag, they might
excite among patriotic people some compassion for my helpless condition,
but I would leave this matter entirely to your judgement.*[4]

Popular historian Walter Lord, in *By the Dawn's Early Light*, his 1972
book about the Battle of Fort McHenry, raised an important question
based on the accounts of eyewitnesses Midshipman Barrett and Private
Munroe. Barrett and Munroe described a flag being hoisted over the fort
on the morning of September 14. Lord suggested that the smaller storm
flag that Mary Pickersgill made might have been flown over the fort during
the wet and windy night of the bombardment, and the larger flag substi-
tuted for it in the morning. This would have been consistent with military
practice of the time. On the other hand, another eyewitness, Mendes I.
Cohen, who was in the fort as an 18-year-old member of Joseph Nicholson's volunteer company, offers a contradictory account. He wrote in 1873,

*I have a full recollection of the damage to the flag by the enemy. . . .
I have a recollection that one whole bomb shell passed through it and
some three or four pieces passed through it. The flag was on a high mast
not far from the bastion I was stationed at on the right side of the star
fort. . . . I do not recollect the size of the flag tho I know it was a very
large one and have only seen it once since then in the possession of
Mr. Hughes Armistead the brother of Mrs. Appleton.*

Georgiana Armistead Appleton, daughter of the defender of Fort McHenry and the guardian of the Star-Spangled Banner from 1861 until her death in 1878. Photograph taken about 1860. Dr. Christopher Hughes Morton, Saddle River, N.J.

Caroline Purdy's mention in her letter to Georgiana Appleton of "rents" in the flag that were "only bound round" appears to corroborate Cohen's account. Also, a witness who examined the flag now at the Smithsonian at Christopher Hughes Armistead's house in 1861 spoke of "eleven holes in it, made there by the shot of the British during the bombardment."

In light of conflicting evidence, it may be that both the large and the small flags may have flown over the fort at different times during the bombardment. The small flag has not been located.[5]

Fifteen Stars and Fifteen Stripes

The design of the flag that Mary Pickersgill and her family made for Fort McHenry in 1813 was the second official version of the American flag.

Credit for the basic design of the first U.S. flag is generally given to Francis Hopkinson (1737–1791), a New Jersey delegate to the Continental Congress, member of the Continental Navy Board, composer, and designer of several government seals. The original Flag Act, passed June 14, 1777, provided that "the flag of the thirteen united States be 13 stripes alternate red and white, that the union be 13 stars, white in a blue field representing a new constellation." The placement of neither the stripes nor the stars was specified, and a wide variety of designs were in use during the early years of the Republic. In some, the blue union ran down the entire hoist of the flag, whereas in others the red and white stripes were in the canton and the stars were in a blue field that occupied the rest of the flag.

Historians can find no documentary evidence to support the popular story that Betsy Ross designed and made the first flag at the request of George Washington in June 1776, a year before Congress passed the original Flag Act. First brought to light in 1870 by Betsy Ross's grandson, William J. Canby, this legend has been repeated often in print since then. The story is usually accompanied by a painting by Charles H. Weisgerber entitled, *The Birth of Our Country's Flag,* which was painted for an exhibition at the World's Columbian Exposition in Chicago in 1893. Betsy Ross was in fact a professional Philadelphia flagmaker and did make a set of flags for Pennsylvania state ships in 1777. Historians view her role in designing and making the first American flag as another cherished myth that has its own place in American history.

Similarly, historians can find no documentary evidence for the symbolism popularly attributed to the flag colors. Nonetheless, Americans find meaning in the belief that red stands for valor; white, for liberty or purity; and blue, for justice, loyalty, and perseverance.

The fifteen stripes and fifteen stars of the Fort McHenry flag reflected a change introduced by the second Flag Act, which was passed January 13, 1794. The act stipulated that after May 1, 1795, the flag design should acknowledge the two new states, Kentucky and Vermont, that had joined the union since the original Flag Act.

The fifteen-star, fifteen-stripe design remained intact from 1794 until 1818, even though additional states continued to join the union after 1795. In 1818 Congressman Peter Wendover of New York introduced a bill based on a proposal from Naval Captain Samuel Chester Reid. The bill would reduce the number of stripes in the flag to thirteen, intended to signify the original thirteen states. It would increase the number of stars to twenty, the number of existing states, while providing that an additional star be added on the admission of each new state.

President James Monroe signed Wendover's bill into law on April 4, 1818, thereby establishing the fundamental design of the present American flag.[6]

4 An Armistead Family Treasure

A JEALOUS AND PERHAPS SELFISH LOVE MADE ME GUARD MY TREASURE WITH WATCHFUL CARE, LEST THE TROPHY OF OUR GALLANT FATHER SHOULD MEET WITH SOME UNTOWARD ACCIDENT.

— Georgiana Armistead Appleton to George Preble,
February 18, 1873

While Key's song was known to virtually every American by the end of the Civil War, the flag that inspired it remained largely a family keepsake, revered by Baltimoreans but unknown outside of that city until the early 1870s.

Sometime before his death on April 25, 1818, Lieutenant Colonel George Armistead acquired the flag that was raised over Fort McHenry as the British ships retreated down the river on the morning of September 14, 1814. Exactly how the flag came into his possession remains somewhat of a mystery. When questioned on the subject in 1873 by naval historian George Preble, Armistead's daughter and namesake, Georgiana Armistead Appleton, said:

I do not know how the flag came into my father's possession — I was not five months old when he died and always accepted the ownership as a fact without question — just as I did any other property. It might have been a usual or granted right for a commander to take a trophy of success. Again it is not unpalpable or improbable that any correspondence on the subject was lost with other valuable papers at the time of the presentation of the sword in Richmond in I think 1839 or 40.

Armistead's granddaughter, Margaret Appleton Baker, said at various times that the flag had been presented to Armistead by the government after the battle. Although this statement has often been repeated in print, historians have never found any documentary evidence to support it. Margaret's brother, Eben Appleton, when pressed about the matter by a committee of Baltimoreans in 1889, said simply that his grandfather "became the owner of the flag" after the bombardment. Correspondence between Appleton and the Smithsonian that has been preserved in the flag's accession file does not address the issue. However, the Smithsonian's 1907 *Annual Report* described the flag as having been "retained by Colonel George Armistead" after the Battle of Fort McHenry.[1]

In the absence of other clear evidence, it would appear that Armistead decided on his own to keep the Star-Spangled Banner after the battle. He clearly appears to have had strong feelings about the flag because he wrote his name in ink, followed by the date "September 14, 1814," on two of the stripes.

The Star-Spangled Banner remained the private possession of George Armistead's widow and descendants for ninety years. During that time, the increasing popularity of Key's anthem and the American public's changing sense of the past transformed the flag from a family keepsake into a national treasure. Its ownership became an increasingly heavy responsibility for Armistead's daughter and for his grandson. It was almost as though the additional layers of significance attached to the flag had literally increased its weight. Eventually the family came to believe that the Star-Spangled Banner belonged in a museum as an artifact of national heritage.

The Banner Displayed

When George Armistead died in 1818, the flag he had fought for at Fort McHenry passed to his widow, Louisa Hughes Armistead. Louisa took care of the flag for nearly forty years, occasionally allowing it to be displayed for patriotic events.

The flag's first documented public appearance since Lieutenant Colonel Armistead's death occurred during the Marquis de Lafayette's October 8, 1824, visit to Baltimore. Louisa Armistead lent it, along with her late husband's presentation silver, to the Society of the Cincinnati for display at a reception for the marquis at Fort McHenry. Signifying the degree of veneration it was already accorded, the flag was displayed along with George Washington's tent and camp chest, which had been borrowed from George Washington Parke Custis for the occasion. A promotional handbill, now at the Maryland Historical Society, described the welcoming ceremonies as follows: "The Banner which waved over Fort McHenry during the memorable bombardment of 1814, having been kindly tendered to the Committee by the relict of the gallant Col. Armistead, will be displayed on the reception of General LA FAYETTE."

Sixty-five years later Baltimorean William Chase Barney recalled, in a letter to the *Baltimore News,* his experiences helping transport the flag to the event. Major William B. Barney, secretary of the Society of the Cincinnati, realized he had forgotten to include the flag in the delivery of Washington's tent and flag. He sent young William Chase Barney in a hack to Mrs. Armistead's residence to get it. The younger Barney also recalled that when it came time to return the flag to Mrs. Armistead, the fort's commander, Colonel James Hindman, resisted, claiming that it was government property. Major Barney had to produce a letter from the War Department before Colonel Hindman would agree to release it.

Fittingly, the Star-Spangled Banner also may have been used to decorate the hall at the Baltimore Athenaeum when a memorial service was held there for General Lafayette on July 4, 1834. The service was organized by the Philocroetian Debating Society, of which Christopher Hughes Armistead was a member. Fifty years after the event, someone recalled to a *Baltimore American* reporter that Christopher Armistead had provided the flag. The flag was also borrowed by the Old Defenders to be displayed at North Point on September 12, 1839, the twenty-fifth anniversary of the battle there. According to a newspaper account of the celebration, the Baltimore Independent Blues, a militia company, marched to Louisa Armistead's house early that morning to receive the flag. They escorted it on the steamboat *Rappahannock* to North Point, where it was hung next to the decorated rostrum from which General B. C. Howard gave an address to the assembled veterans. The *Baltimore American* reported on Howard's speech as follows:

> *The particulars of the bombardment of Fort McHenry were detailed, and a just eulogy was pronounced upon the gallant conduct of the brave men who repelled the enemy's fleet from both branches of the Patapsco. The identical flag which streamed amid the flames and smoke of the bombardment, and which bore evidences of the strife by the holes made through it by the shells, hung waving in front of the speaker. He made a beautiful allusion to it in connexion with those celebrated verses entitled the "Star Spangled Banner," which were written on that memorable occasion, and which now have become consecrated as part of our National music. The oration was followed by a dinner for the*

Blues and their guests on board the Rappahannock, *after which they returned to Baltimore and marched once more to Mrs. Armistead's house to return the flag.*[2]

When Francis Scott Key died in January 1843, Mrs. Armistead's brother-in-law, Colonel Samuel Moore, offered Key's family the use of the Star-Spangled Banner for his funeral procession. It would appear that the Key family declined, however, as there was no mention of the flag in the newspaper accounts of his funeral. The flag went on display again in May 1844, when the Young Men's Whig National Convention was held in Baltimore. A pamphlet describing the decorations and the processions that wound through the streets beneath them stated, "From the premises of Christopher Hughes Armistead, just above Charles Street, was displayed the identical Star Spangled Banner which waved over Fort McHenry on the night of the bombardment by the British in 1814; whose waving through 'that perilous night' suggested the thought of that most beautiful of all our National songs — The Star Spangled Banner."[3]

Handed Down, Mother to Daughter

Before Louisa Armistead died on October 3, 1861, she bequeathed the Star-Spangled Banner that had signaled her husband's triumph at the 1814 Battle of Fort McHenry to her daughter Georgiana Armistead Appleton. The silver service that had been presented to George Armistead by the grateful citizens of Baltimore went to her son, Christopher Hughes Armistead. Although Christopher Hughes Armistead was disappointed by his mother's decision, his wife, Agnes Gordon Armistead, apparently was glad to be relieved of what she considered to be a burden. A Gordon family story quotes her as having said, "More battles have been fought over that flag than were ever fought under it, and I, for one, am glad to be rid of it!"[4]

In 1873, seeking to explain to naval historian George Henry Preble the flag's location during the Civil War, Georgiana Armistead Appleton also speculated why she and not her brother had inherited the flag:

> At the breaking out of the war it [the flag] was in our house but Mr. Appleton immediately broke up housekeeping and our furniture was stored. The flag was then taken for safekeeping to my brother's house in Monument Street, and my mother shortly after went (most unwillingly) with him and his family to Virginia, where she shortly after died, but on his return he was, after some angry words for he thought the flag should have been his, forced to give it up to me and with me it has remained ever since, loved and venerated. . . . Her reasons were that I was called after my father and was the only one of his children born at Fort McHenry. There is a legend that at the time of my birth this banner was raised and the disappointment was great that I was a girl.[5]

The youngest child of George and Louisa Armistead, Georgiana was born at Fort McHenry on November 25, 1817. She married William Stuart Appleton on November 27, 1838. A well-connected Bostonian, Appleton was the son of Eben Appleton, one of the founders of the Lowell, Massachusetts, textile mills, and the nephew of Nathan Appleton, a Boston textile manufacturer and sometime congressman from Massachusetts. After their marriage, the Appletons lived in Baltimore, where he was in the commission and banking business. They had ten children, seven of whom survived to adulthood.

Secessionist Sentiments

Despite her husband's Boston connections, Georgiana Appleton was a Southern sympathizer in a city that remained part of the union and was full of Federal troops during the Civil War. In 1861 her son George

Armistead Appleton was imprisoned as part of a group of young men who had been trying to go to Virginia to join the Confederate Army. Arrested before he could fight against the nation that his grandfather and namesake had fought to defend, he was held at — of all places — Fort McHenry. Georgiana wrote a letter to her son that unabashedly set forth her Southern sympathies:

> *I say it is an outrage that you should be left a prisoner. . . . I have no ill or personal feelings for any of my friends who differ in personal opinion from me. I have (thank God) no drop of Puritan blood in my body and therefore can be as tolerant as I am and beside that the South can be magnanimous at all times and more particularly now. . . . You know Baltimore the beautiful is empty of men . . . all the "Rowdies" have enlisted in the Federal Army and all the gentlemen, God save the mark, are in Virginia.*[6]

The Appletons probably kept the Star-Spangled Banner in their Baltimore home during the Civil War. Margaret Appleton Baker told a reporter for the *New York Herald* in 1895 that "during the Civil War the flag was sent out of the country, I believe to England, as the city of Baltimore was at that time any but a safe place to remain in." However, no evidence supports her recollection, which would also seem to contradict her mother's 1873 response to naval historian George Preble's question about the flag's location during the war.[7]

Modifications to the Flag

In the antiquarian tradition of relic worship — the veneration of pieces of significant historical objects — Louisa Armistead permitted a number of people to cut small pieces from her flag. Armistead family tradition holds that the first piece was removed to be buried with one of the veterans of the bombardment at the request of a grieving widow. Louisa Armistead's daughter, Georgiana Armistead Appleton, wrote in 1873: "Pieces of the flag have occasionally been given to those who deemed to have a right to such a memento — indeed had we have given all that we had been importuned for little would be left to show." She added that "the star was cut out for some official person" but did not say who that was. One legend sometimes stated in print tells that the star was given to Abraham Lincoln at the beginning of the Civil War, but neither the Lincoln Papers nor any other documentary source reveals any evidence that he received it. Considering the Armisteads' Southern sympathies, the story seems highly unlikely.

Georgiana Appleton continued the practice of giving away fragments of the Star-Spangled Banner, and by the time it came to the Smithsonian in 1907, eight feet of material were missing from the fly end. The few fragments that have been donated to the Smithsonian over the years are in the collections of the National Museum of American History.

Another modification made to the flag was the addition of the red chevron onto the third white stripe from the bottom of the flag. Louisa Armistead sewed on this feature, which, according to Georgiana Appleton, was intended to be the letter *A,* presumably for Armistead. A small, embroidered letter *B,* the significance of which is unknown, appears on the chevron. Louisa Armistead may have intended to sew the entire Armistead name onto the stripe, as names of political candidates and even commercial enterprises were commonly printed on the white stripes of American flags in the 1840s and 1850s.[8]

Toward a National Symbol

The popularity of the song "The Star-Spangled Banner" during the Civil War also renewed interest in the flag that was its subject. Indeed, historians began to take an interest in the flag at about the same time that its ownership passed to Georgiana Appleton in 1861. This interest led Georgiana to realize that the flag had a national significance that transcended its status as a family treasure.

An Armistead family member informed historian Benson J. Lossing of the flag's existence in 1861 while Lossing was researching his *Pictorial Field-Book of the War of 1812*. Lossing traveled to Baltimore and found the flag at Christopher Hughes Armistead's house. He described his visit in his magazine, *The American Historical Record*:

> *I called upon Mr. Christopher Hughes Armistead, son of Colonel George Armistead, the commander of Fort McHenry in 1814, who kindly showed me the identical flag of which Key inquired "O, say, does that star spangled banner yet wave o'er the land of the free and the home of the brave?" Mr. Armistead spread it out on his parlor floor. It was the regular garrison flag faded and worn by exposure to storms and missiles. It had eleven holes in it, made there by the shot of the British during the bombardment of Fort McHenry.*[9]

In 1872 Commodore (later Rear Admiral) George Henry Preble brought out the first edition of his massive work *Our Flag: Origin of the Flag of the United States of America*. Preble was unaware, however, of the true history of the actual Star-Spangled Banner. He quoted an unnamed informant as saying that he had been shown the original flag at Fort McHenry in 1852 "rolled up in a piece of dirty muslin and thrown into a corner covered with dust."

After reading that passage in February 1873, Georgiana Appleton wrote Preble the first of fourteen letters about the flag. In that first letter she outlined the history of the flag's ownership since her father's death in 1818 — emphasizing that the flag had not been at Fort McHenry in 1852 — as follows:

Had the flag been at Fort McHenry during the rebellion, would not the government have produced it, as the watchword of Union and Liberty? Even then it was mine, and a jealous and perhaps selfish love made me guard my treasure with watchful care, lest this trophy of our gallant father should meet with some untoward accident.

Appleton also shared with Preble her change of heart regarding the flag's ownership, stating,

Now I have come to look at the matter in a different light and I think this time honored relic should not remain in private hands, but that it should be in some public place, where our sons and daughters might be taught to look at and love this labarum [standard] of our country.[10]

Preble responded immediately to Georgiana Appleton, asking if he could have a photograph of the flag, along with an account of the flag's history as she remembered it, to include in the next edition of his book. She agreed and in June 1873 shipped the flag by railway express to Preble's office at the Boston Navy Yard so he could photograph it. Preble had a canvas backing stitched to the flag. On June 21 he hung the newly backed flag on the side of a building, where he took the first known photographs of the Star-Spangled Banner. As he wrote to Mrs. Appleton, "I have had the Glorious Old Flag quilted to a sail — and so it was hung out from the 2nd story of one of the buildings at the Navy Yard yesterday afternoon and successfully photographed. I obtained from Col. Jones a couple of Marine privates to stand in full dress and be photographed with it to show by comparison its size, and at the same time serve as a guard of honor for the honorable and historic relic." He later said that he had intended to have the flag hoisted on the Navy Yard flagstaff and have a twenty-one gun salute fired to it. He said he soon realized that the "Glorious Old Flag" would be too fragile for that honor.[11]

The first known photograph of the Star-Spangled Banner, taken at the Boston Navy Yard, June 21, 1873. American Antiquarian Society, Worcester, Mass.

As the nation's leading authority on the history of the American flag, Commodore Preble quickly became the publicist who placed the Star-Spangled Banner on a national stage. When the flag arrived at the Navy Yard, he wrote an article about it for the *Boston Transcript*. On July 9, 1873, he exhibited the flag at the headquarters of the New England Historic Genealogical Society in Boston along with the flag that had flown on the brig *Enterprise* during her action with the British brig *Boxer* in 1813 and the colors said to have been flown by John Paul Jones's ship, *Bonhomme Richard*. Preble gave a public lecture entitled, "Three Historic Flags and Three September Victories," which he later had printed as a pamphlet.

With Mrs. Appleton's permission, Preble clipped some fragments — he called them "snippings" — from the flag and sent them to friends in the antiquarian world along with copies of the pamphlet and prints, mounted on stiff cardboard, of his photograph of the flag. He also persuaded Georgiana Appleton to send photographs of the Rembrandt Peale portrait of her father to some of the recipients.[12]

After Preble's lecture and exhibition, the flag was placed in the vault of the New England Historic and Genealogical Society. In January 1876 it was moved to the vault of the Historical Society of Pennsylvania, from which it was to have been transported to the Philadelphia Centennial Exhibition for display. It is doubtful that the flag was ever displayed at the Philadelphia Centennial Exhibition. In March 1873, before the flag even went to Preble in Boston, Charles B. Norton of the U.S. Centennial Commission, presumably alerted by Preble, wrote to Georgiana Appleton. He asked if she was interested in exhibiting the flag at the Centennial Exhibition. Nine months later, Georgiana Appleton's Baltimore girlhood friend, Alice Taney Campbell Etting, also wrote, explaining that she and her husband Frank Etting were founding a "National Museum" in Independence Hall in Philadelphia, scheduled to open at the same time as the Centennial Exhibition. She said that she would be presenting a copy of a letter describing her uncle Francis Scott Key's "excursion on which he wrote the 'Star-Spangled Banner'" to the museum and added, "I am very anxious to have the original flag deposited for a while in Independence Hall and write to ask if you will not loan it to us."

On Preble's advice, Georgiana Appleton decided not to lend the flag to the Ettings' National Museum but rather to place it in the Navy Department exhibit being assembled by Admiral Thornton Jenkins for the Philadelphia Centennial Exhibition.[13]

Admiral Jenkins signed a receipt for the flag, dated January 10, 1876. No evidence exists that he actually displayed the flag, however, even though it is listed in the catalogue of the Navy Department exhibit. In July 1876 Preble wrote to Georgiana Appleton:

> I visited the Exhibition many times — I found your flag had not been displayed and had a talk with Admiral Jenkins about it who said he had been afraid to put it up fearing it would be mutilated but promised at my suggestion to put it up overhead and out of reach and suitably inscribed — I afterwards wrote him and received in reply a short note saying it would be displayed [with] a printed card in three languages describing it as a relic.

The flag did not go on display, however, and the next month Preble wrote Mrs. Appleton to say that he had been "very much annoyed at the non-display." In September she wrote back, asking for Admiral Jenkins's address and stating, "I now intend to have my banner again in my own keeping. Had I known it could not have been worn at the Exhibition I should have loaned it to Mr. Etting."[14]

A year or so before the Centennial Exhibition opened, Georgiana Appleton evidently had considered presenting her flag to a specific public institution. In November 1875, her husband's cousin Nathan

Appleton, Jr., wrote to her saying, "I write now to ask you what are your plans about the Star-Spangled Banner, of which you know we have often talked, that is whether you still think of presenting it to the people of the United States, and allowing me to be the medium of presentation, at some great national fete day as for instance the Fourth of July next and at Philadelphia. . . . I would like as I have told you to have the orating part of the programme."[15]

A connection may exist between these conversations with Nathan Appleton and a handwritten inscription on one of the flag's stars, which reads, "This precious relic of my father's fame I . . . ." The part of the inscription following the word *I* has been cut out with scissors, and below the hole are the signature "Georgiana Armistead Appleton" and the date "July 24, 1876." Mrs. Appleton may have intended to present her flag to the nation during the Philadelphia Centennial Exhibition. She may have then changed her mind, as a result of Admiral Jenkins's "non-display" of the flag.

On June 14, 1877, during the nation's first Flag Day celebration, Georgiana Appleton agreed to exhibit her flag at the Old South Church in Boston, and Nathan Appleton, Jr., got his opportunity to orate during the nation's first Flag Day celebration. Flags were displayed all over the city, but the celebration focused on the Old South Church, where the Star-Spangled Banner was displayed along with two other historic flags. The Mayor of Boston, Frederick O. Prince, served as chairman of the program, and Nathan Appleton, Jr., was the principal speaker.

Nathan Appleton began with an account of the bombardment of Fort McHenry that drew heavily upon Roger B. Taney's letter describing Key's writing of "The Star-Spangled Banner." He summarized the history of flags in general and the development of the U.S. flag in particular. He further quoted several patriotic poems about the American flag, referred to the task of consolidating the Union after the Civil War, and closed by saying that he wished that every citizen could gaze upon the flag that was there beside the speaker's rostrum. Specifically he cited the flag's "simple beauty [to] show mankind, as has never been done before, that social, political, and religious liberty can go hand in hand together."[16]

In the last quarter of the nineteenth century, the Star-Spangled Banner rose substantially in monetary value along with its fame. Despite a severe downturn in her financial situation, Georgiana Appleton resisted offers to buy the flag. As she wrote to George Preble, "In heavy reverses of fortune when friends have suggested that I might perhaps sell it [the flag] for a high price accepting the overtures that were made for its purchase — I have felt that I would rather beg than part with my treasure."

William Stuart Appleton's business had failed at the beginning of the Civil War, and neither he nor their sons could find employment in Baltimore. Georgiana described her condition as "destitute and suffering" until her husband's uncle Nathan Appleton established a trust fund for her and their children in April 1861. William Stuart Appleton wrote to thank his uncle, saying that he could "only endeavor in the years that remain to me be they few or many to retrieve the property and position that I have lost. My prospects are certainly not very cheering."

Eventually William Stuart Appleton found employment at the Collector of Customs Office in New York, but as late as 1876 Georgiana was still referring in her correspondence with George Preble to their financial difficulties. She seems to have maintained a kind of philosophical humor amid what were actually rather dire straits. She once wrote Preble about a relative named Mary B. Carter, indicating that she had forgotten whether the "B." stood for "Bowles or Beverly for we are related to both families but not B, the Bankers!"[17]

A Heavy Responsibility

The flag that Eben Appleton inherited on his mother's death on July 25, 1878, had become far more than a family keepsake. The publicity it had received in the 1870s transformed it into a national treasure.

Eben Appleton was, in fact, an extremely private man and shunned the inquiries and, ultimately, notoriety that his ownership of the Star-Spangled Banner brought him. He locked the flag in a safe-deposit vault in downtown Manhattan and refused to disclose its location.

Appleton had no sooner locked up the flag than he received the first of what he later remembered to be at least twenty requests to lend his relic to a civic celebration. This first request came from his native city, Baltimore, where the City Council was planning to lay the cornerstone to the Eutaw Street monument to George Armistead as part of its five-day Sesquicentennial celebration being planned for October 1880. In view of the honor being paid to his grandfather, Appleton agreed to bring the flag to Baltimore.

On October 13, 1880, the Star-Spangled Banner was carried through the streets of Baltimore as part of a military parade led by two artillery batteries and a company of infantry from Fort McHenry. The fort's twenty-two-piece band and a contingent of sailors and marines from the U.S.S. *Kearsage* and the U.S.S. *Vandalia* followed. A decorated carriage drove behind them, carrying nine of the remaining Old Defenders — men in their eighties and nineties dressed in black dress suits and top hats. One of these surviving heroes, Henry Lightner, carried a battered kettledrum in his arms. The carriage was escorted by a color guard of Grand Army of the Republic veterans. Behind, in another carriage, came the Star-Spangled Banner, folded in the lap of William W. Carter, a local historian and proponent of the Armistead monument. Militia companies and volunteer firemen from all over Maryland, their horse-drawn engines decked with flowers, brought up the rear. A newspaper account of the parade indicated that "as the tattered old relic was seen by the crowds, their enthusiasm was unbounded."

This parade was the last time that the Star-Spangled Banner was seen in Baltimore. But as the flag was being packed for shipment back to New York, Appleton invited Carter to snip three fragments — one red, one white, and one blue — from the 67-year-old flag. Carter framed the pieces and presented them to the Maryland Historical Society. In 1926 the society donated the objects to the Smithsonian Institution.[18]

Eben Appleton took quite seriously his responsibility as a trustee of a national treasure. In 1889 he declined to lend the flag to a committee of Baltimoreans who were planning a five-day celebration of the seventy-fifth anniversary of the bombardment. Appleton felt that the occasion, which included an agricultural and industrial arts fair, lacked

The Old Defenders at Druid Hill Park, Baltimore, October 1880. Maryland Historical Society, Baltimore

the decorum befitting the flag. There followed a series of misunder-standings not only about the nature of the celebration but also about the way in which the flag would be displayed. A rift developed between Appleton and Francis P. Stevens, the committee chairman. Stevens announced to the Baltimore press that the flag had always been govern-ment property, that it did not legally belong to Appleton, and that he intended to see the Secretary of War and force Appleton to give it up.

A committee headed by Stevens did call on the Acting Secretary of War, General Robert Macfeely, who sent a tactful letter to Appleton that did not raise the matter of ownership but simply suggested that Appleton "should be pleased to comply with the reasonable request of the citizens of Baltimore." Appleton wrote a polite reply, saying that to lend the flag under the circumstances would be inconsistent with his duty toward the preservation of the flag. He cited the flag's poor con-dition and the depredations of relic hunters and also expressed the opinion that the Baltimore celebration was not "an occasion of great national interest."

Privately Eben Appleton was enraged at the suggestion that the flag was not legally his and at the action of the committee in approach-ing General Macfeely. A reporter for the *Baltimore American* described an interview in Appleton's New York home during which the flag's keeper gestured toward a picture of his grandfather and said, "Does that look like the face of a man who would claim property not his own?" To add insult to injury, the committee visited Appleton's home at 71 East 54th Street to renew their plea. Appleton responded em-phatically that the flag would not be made available to them. At a second meeting the next day at the Astor House hotel, Appleton remained adamant and refused to disclose the location of the flag, which was still in its safe-deposit vault.

Meanwhile, a group of Baltimore ladies, who were descendants of the Old Defenders, announced that, in view of Appleton's refusal to send the flag to Baltimore, they intended to create a full-size replica of it for use at the celebration. On September 8 Miss Adah Schley presented the replica — along with some unkind remarks about Appleton — to the Mayor of Baltimore. This incident and the publicity it received in the Baltimore and New York newspapers upset Appleton tremendously. According to his sister, Georgiana Appleton Hunter, he refused for the next eighteen years to discuss the flag or to disclose his address, "having been much annoyed about his heirloom all of his life."[19]

When he entered his early sixties, Eben Appleton began to address his concerns about the flag's future. He had no male heirs. Looking beyond his family, he approached the national museum, the Smithsonian Institution in Washington, D.C.

5 The Star-Spangled Banner and the Smithsonian Institution

IT HAS ALWAYS BEEN MY INTENTION TO PRESENT THE FLAG DURING MY LIFETIME TO THAT INSTITUTION IN THE COUNTRY WHERE IT COULD BE CONVENIENTLY SEEN BY THE PUBLIC, AND WHERE IT WOULD BE WELL CARED FOR, AND THE ADVANTAGES AND APPROPRIATENESS OF THE NATIONAL MUSEUM ARE SO OBVIOUS, AS TO RENDER THE CONSIDERATION OF ANY OTHER PLACE UNNECESSARY.

— Eben Appleton to Smithsonian Secretary Charles Walcott, December 12, 1912

Eben Appleton lent the Star-Spangled Banner to the Smithsonian Institution in 1907. In 1912 he converted the loan to a gift. On January 10, 1914, he wrote to Smithsonian secretary Charles Walcott, saying, "I . . . congratulate myself daily upon it being in such competent hands, and anything you may deem best to be done for its preservation and display will always have my hearty approval."

The Star-Spangled Banner displayed for a photograph on the Smithsonian Institution Building on the day that it arrived at the Smithsonian, July 1907. Smithsonian Institution, Washington, D.C.

Since receiving the flag, the Smithsonian has displayed it to the public. In 1907 it was mounted in a large exhibit case in the Arts and Industries Building. After the National Museum of History and Technology (now the National Museum of American History) opened in 1964, it was hung in the museum's Flag Hall. There, it looked down on inaugural balls, presidential speeches, and other public ceremonies, and was admired by millions of Americans. In 1998 the flag was placed in a special laboratory to undergo a major preservation effort.

Over the years, the Smithsonian has labored to preserve the Star-Spangled Banner for future generations.

A Gift to the National Museum

In 1907, when Eben Appleton decided to unburden himself of his treasure, he first corresponded with both the Governor of Maryland and the Mayor of Baltimore about donating the flag to the state or the city. Soon after, Appleton was approached by a history-minded cousin, John B. Baylor, employed by the U.S. Coast and Geodetic Survey and an acquaintance of Smithsonian Secretary Charles D. Walcott.

Baylor wrote to Walcott, describing his kinship to Appleton and asking Walcott to "second my efforts to convince Mr. Appleton to either lend or give his flag to the National Museum." "If you handle him in a tactful manner," Baylor said, "I believe he will do this." Baylor enclosed a letter he had received from Appleton saying that the National Museum at the Smithsonian appealed to him more than any other option for placing the flag. Walcott replied immediately to Baylor, saying, "The addition of this notable object to the historical collections of the National Museum would be very deeply appreciated," and that "it would be acceptable either as a loan or a gift, and would be given a conspicuous position such as it deserves."

Baylor passed along Secretary Walcott's letter to Appleton, who then wrote to Walcott. Appleton stated that he had often thought it would be a good idea to exhibit the flag "in one of the public buildings in Washington" and asked for more information about the Institution and its policies.

By June 30 Appleton had decided to lend the flag to the Smithsonian. He asked only to be reassured that the Smithsonian would not in turn lend the flag to any third party without his consent. Packed in the wooden crate that Commodore Preble had made for it in 1876, the flag was shipped from New York by Adams Express on July 5, 1907, and arrived at the Smithsonian the next day. Secretary Walcott was out of town when it came, but Assistant Secretary Richard Rathbun had it hung on the exterior wall of the Smithsonian Institution building, now the "Castle." The flag was then placed in a case in the Arts and Industries building's Hall of History, next to cases holding military artifacts that had belonged to George Washington and Ulysses S. Grant. Rathbun wrote Appleton that "[the Star-Spangled Banner's] presence in the museum has caused a wave of patriotism, which it is very good to see." The exceptionally large flag had to be folded a number of times to fit into the case.[1]

In 1912 Eben Appleton decided to convert the loan to a gift. The only condition that he attached at that time was that the Smithsonian display an exhibit label near the flag that identified it as the flag that was defended by Colonel George Armistead and his men and that inspired Francis Scott Key to write the verses of "The Star-Spangled Banner." A year later Appleton added the condition that the flag not leave the Smithsonian under any circumstances. The event that precipitated this stipulation was an attempt by the National Star-Spangled Banner Centennial Commission in Baltimore to have the flag brought to Baltimore for their September 1914 celebration.

The Baltimore commission's request began in December 1913, when Arthur A. Bibbins, chair of the Centennial Commission, called on Secretary Walcott and proposed that the Smithsonian restore the flag and then lend it to the centennial celebration. Walcott consulted with Assistant Secretary Rathbun, who told him that the flag could never be restored to a condition that would permit it to travel. He said specifically, "If taken away it would most likely fall to pieces." Walcott conveyed this observation to Bibbins in a polite letter, in which he also stated that the Smithsonian had recently refused to lend the flag to the Toledo Museum of Art. He said the Smithsonian would also have to decline to lend it to Baltimore.

In the meantime, Bibbins had written directly to Eben Appleton, asking him to use his influence with Secretary Walcott to have the Smithsonian transfer the flag's ownership to the City of Baltimore, to be permanently displayed in a memorial hall to be built at Fort McHenry. Horrified, Appleton fired off a letter to Walcott, asking what he might do to prevent the Smithsonian from ever lending or donating the flag. He said he had given the flag to the Smithsonian "with practically no condition attached to the gift, because I could not conceive of the authorities donating to any one or any place anything which had been given to them." Walcott reassured him that, if he so desired, the flag would never leave the museum, even temporarily. He asked Appleton for a letter specifically stating that condition. Appleton wrote back on January 10, 1914, saying, "I gave the flag to the National Museum with the firm and settled intention of having it remain there forever and regarded the acceptance of the gift by the Authorities of the Museum as an evidence of their willingness to comply with this condition, and I could not for one moment consent to its transfer to any other place, even temporarily."[2]

In spite of this unequivocal statement, Arthur Bibbins and the National Star-Spangled Banner Centennial Commission pursued their request for the loan of the flag with the Secretary of War, the House Committee on Military Affairs, and Eben Appleton's own daughter,

Mrs. William E. Morton. So certain was the Commission of its success that it printed a statement in the program for the Star-Spangled Banner Centennial Celebration that the original Star-Spangled Banner was to be carried in a Baltimore parade on September 12, 1914.

On August 31, 1914, Appleton proclaimed to Walcott, "Therefore, let us all stand firm at *this time* and at *all* times, and under *all* circumstances, and let any American citizen who visits the museum with the expectation of seeing the flag be sure of finding it in its accustomed place." He described the pressure that was being brought upon him and his determination not to give in to it.[3]

Both Eben Appleton and the Smithsonian Institution did stand firm, and the flag has been on view for many generations of Smithsonian visitors.

"Just Fading Away"

From the day that the flag arrived at the Smithsonian Institution building on the National Mall, Smithsonian officials recognized that it was in delicate condition. As early as 1873, Georgiana Appleton had described the flag as "just fading away, being among our earthly treasures where moth and rust must corrupt."[4]

In 1907 Assistant Secretary Richard Rathbun wrote to Eben Appleton that the flag's canvas backing was too heavy for it and that he might suggest a new backing. Soon after he met with Secretary Walcott in December 1913, chair of the Baltimore Centennial Commission Arthur Bibbins mentioned to Secretary Walcott that the historic flag collection at the Naval Academy in Annapolis had been preserved by Amelia Fowler, of Boston. Bibbins suggested that Fowler might do the same for the Star-Spangled Banner.

Early in February 1914, Theodore Belote, a Smithsonian Assistant Curator of History, was dispatched to Annapolis to look at the Naval

Academy flags. He enthusiastically reported his findings and explained Mrs. Fowler's preservation method, which involved stitching each flag to a linen backing with a net stitch. Belote recommended that the Smithsonian retain Fowler to treat the Star-Spangled Banner in the same way so that "it would then be feasible to suspend it lengthwise on the west wall of the North Hall with the Union in the upper left corner."[5]

On March 25, 1914, Rathbun wrote to Mrs. Fowler asking for her terms for sewing a new backing to the Star-Spangled Banner. Almost exactly a hundred years after Mary Pickersgill and her family made the flag in Baltimore, the first steps to preserve it were taken.[6]

Amelia Bold Fowler was a Boston teacher of embroidery who became involved in flag preservation in 1900, when she advised the State of Massachusetts on the preservation of the Civil War flags displayed at the State House in Boston. In 1912 she and a team of forty needlewomen she had trained were retained by the U.S. Naval Academy to preserve a collection of 172 historic flags. From that work she developed a method of preservation that she patented in 1913. This method involved laying a flag — or in some cases the remaining pieces of a flag — out on a piece of unbleached Irish or Belgian linen that was cut to the size of the flag. The flag was then ironed flat with an electric iron and stitched to the linen backing with an interlocking network of stitches that formed a mesh of thread over the face of the flag, holding it to the backing with about twelve stitches per square inch. Before being stitched into place, the thread was carefully dyed to match the portion of the flag that it would cover so that the resulting mesh would blend in with the flag.[7]

Mrs. Fowler agreed to do the work on the Star-Spangled Banner under a government contract for a total fee of $1,243, which included $243 for materials, $500 to pay a team of ten needlewomen, and a $500 fee for herself. Fowler's team laid out the flag on a set of makeshift tables in the room in the "Castle" then known as the chapel (now the

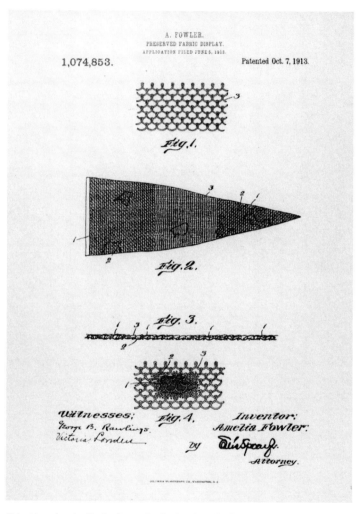

Patent issued to Amelia Fowler on October 7, 1913, for "new and useful improvements in preserved fabric display," U.S. Patent and Trademark Office, Washington, D.C.

Amelia Fowler and her team of needlewomen sew the new linen support to the Star-Spangled Banner in the Smithsonian Institution Building, 1914. Smithsonian Institution, Washington, D.C.

Smithsonian Commons), where Horatio Greenough's seated statue of George Washington was displayed. The needlewomen removed the canvas backing that Commodore Preble's sailors had sewn on in 1873 and sewed on a new linen backing using approximately 1,700,000 stitches. They sewed the linen backing to the same side of the flag that the canvas backing had been on. This meant that when the flag was displayed in a horizontal position, the union was on the viewer's right, rather than on the left as required by the Flag Code passed by the National Flag Conference in 1923. After this deviation was repeatedly pointed out by visitors over the years, the Smithsonian eventually added a label explaining that the flag was backed and mounted before the passage of the Flag Code.

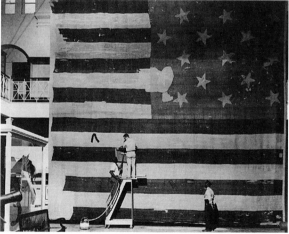

TOP: *The Star-Spangled Banner in its case at the Smithsonian Institution's Arts and Industries Building, 1949. Photograph by B. Anthony Stewart, National Geographic Society.* BOTTOM: *Smithsonian staff vacuuming the Star-Spangled Banner in the Arts and Industries Building, 1950s. Smithsonian Institution, Washington, D.C.*

Amelia Fowler and her team completed their work in eight weeks between mid-May and mid-July 1914, in Mrs. Fowler's words, "with Greenough's marble statue of Washington gravely observing . . . from its place at the end of the room."

The newly backed flag was mounted in a horizontal position in a specially constructed case on the west wall of the north hall of the Arts and Industries Building, just to the right of the main entrance to the building. Although the case was nearly 17 feet high and 35 feet long, it was not tall enough for the entire flag to be displayed and so the lower half was folded up in the bottom of the case. A layer of naphthalene flakes in the bottom of the case protected its contents from insect damage. Only the blue union and its stars and the top half of the stripes were visible to visitors.[8]

In 1921 George Armistead's great-grandson, Alexander Gordon, presented the Smithsonian with the silver service that the citizens of Baltimore had bestowed on George Armistead in 1816. The Smithsonian placed the set in a case next to the flag.

Except for two years between November 1942 and November 1944, when the Star-Spangled Banner was sent to a government warehouse in Shenandoah National Park near Luray, Virginia, to protect it from possible bombing raids, the Star-Spangled Banner remained on exhibit in its case at the Arts and Industries Building. In September 1961 Smithsonian staff took down the flag to prepare it for its move to the new National Museum of History and Technology, now the National Museum of American History.[9]

The Flag Hall

The Star-Spangled Banner figured prominently in planning for the Smithsonian's new National Museum of History and Technology in the 1950s and early 1960s. In the late 1950s, the architect Walker Cain, of the architectural firm of McKim, Meade and White, conceived of a three-story Flag Hall in which to display the flag mounted vertically in a place of honor at the center of the museum. The monumental space faced the entrance to the National Mall and would accommodate display of the entire Star-Spangled Banner for the first time since its arrival at the Smithsonian in 1907. The flag itself would be in a recess lined with glazed blue tiles and surrounded by a proscenium.

To prepare the flag for its new vertical mounting, workers laid out the flag on tables in the third-floor service court of the Arts and Industries Building. Specially woven two-inch-wide linen tapes were sewn at ten-inch intervals to Mrs. Fowler's linen backing. After the tapes were sewn on, the flag was returned to its case, where it remained until December 1963, when it was carefully folded into a truck and driven across the Mall to its new home.[10]

Once in its new exhibition space, the flag was mounted on a forty-foot-high framework of three-inch metal tubing erected within the recess. The linen tapes on the flag's backing were affixed to a pipe at the top of the frame, and additional linen strips were sewn to the sides of the flag and safety-pinned to the diamond-patterned metal grid that covered the outer surface of the framework. The flag was protected from dust by a curtain of filtered air, which was blown in front of its entire surface from air diffusers that ran down the walls on either side of the recess. A false fly end with red and white stripes dyed to match the corresponding stripes on the flag was attached to the grid below the flag's ragged fly end, leaving the visual impression of the intact original flag. Visitors who entered the museum from the Mall entrance saw the flag towering in front of them as they came through the doors, and school groups who arrived through the first-floor bus entrance saw it slowly revealed to them as they ascended an escalator. Either way one entered, the effect was dramatic.

For the next thirty-four years, the Star-Spangled Banner not only greeted visitors but also served as a backdrop for inaugural balls, Presidential visits, naturalization ceremonies, and other grand events held in the Flag Hall.

Protecting and Preserving the Flag

As the Smithsonian stayed abreast of increasing scientific knowledge about textile conservation, staff members cited flaws in the Flag Hall's display system. The air curtain did not maintain the desired levels of temperature and humidity, and the difficult-to-maintain lighting system created light levels that were deemed too high for the health of the flag. Furthermore, periodic inspections revealed a buildup of dust on the flag's surface.

In January 1981 the Museum initiated a two-year conservation project. The flag was carefully examined, and conservators working from scaffolding vacuumed both its back and front surfaces. The area behind the flag was modified to reduce dust accumulation, and new lighting and air-handling systems were installed. From the visitor's point of view, the most important change was the installation of an opaque screen in front of the flag that was lowered once every hour to the accompaniment of a short sound production of two nineteenth-century arrangements of "The Star-Spangled Banner" played on historic band instruments and a brief narrative history of the flag. At these hourly intervals, visitors caught a brief but dramatic glimpse of the flag. From a conservation point of view, the screen protected the flag from excessive exposure to light, dirt, and dust.[11]

In 1994 the mechanism that operated the protective screen failed, and rather than reinstall it the museum took the opportunity to undertake a complete reevaluation of the flag's condition, with a view of preserving it far into the future. In November 1996, a conference of

Conservators cleaning the face of the flag at the National Museum of American History, 1982. Smithsonian Institution, Washington, D.C.

fifty flag historians and conservation experts met for two days at the museum to discuss methods of preservation and exhibition. Following that conference an international technical advisory committee on the preservation of the flag was created. The museum's conservators and curators mapped out a plan to remove harmful soils from the flag's surface, attach it to new support materials to replace those that had been weakened by time, stabilize the environment in which it is exhibited, and provide for its care in the future. In the summer of 1998 the Star-Spangled Banner Preservation Project became part of the "Save America's Treasures" program, a public-private project of the White House Millennium Council and the National Trust for Historic Preservation. On July 13, 1998, President Bill Clinton, First Lady Hillary

Rodham Clinton, and Ralph Lauren visited the National Museum of American History to announce the $10 million contribution from Polo Ralph Lauren to the flag's conservation through the "Save America's Treasures" Program. Generous support for the preservation project was also provided by The Pew Charitable Trusts, which pledged $5 million; a $3 million congressional appropriation; and additional support from The John S. and James L. Knight Foundation, as well as by donations from hundreds of individuals.[12]

In December 1998 the flag was taken down from its mountings and lowered into a temporary laboratory constructed in the Flag Hall. During the previous month it had been photographed with a near-infrared camera provided by the National Aeronautics and Space Administration. Once in the temporary laboratory it was photographed again, this time with equipment provided by Hasselblad USA Incorporated. The purpose of the near-infrared photography was to reveal areas of weakness in the flag's fibers. The second set of pictures was assembled into a detailed map of the flag's surface. Both sides of the flag were carefully examined and vacuumed by conservators working from a movable bridge that spanned the flag's surface. That examination revealed that the dyes in the network of stitches that Amelia Fowler's needlewomen had sewn over the flag had faded badly and that the linen backing had weakened with age.

The flag was then rolled onto a 35-foot-long cylinder and moved into a specially constructed 2,000-square-foot laboratory on the second floor of the museum. The laboratory's plate glass windows permitted conservation treatment to be conducted under the eyes of visitors. This treatment will help to ensure that, when the project is completed, the Star-Spangled Banner will inspire future generations.

Visitors who see the Star-Spangled Banner at the National Museum of American History share a moment of the past with Francis Scott Key,

Lieutenant Colonel George Armistead, and all of those people in the succeeding generations who have treasured this great flag and helped to preserve it. Its broad stripes and bright stars, although somewhat faded, still remind us of that September morning in 1814 when Key wrote the words that are now so familiar to all of us.

The patches and inscriptions on the flag's surface speak of the meaning that this flag had for the Armistead family and for the people of Baltimore. The missing pieces tell of its slow transformation into a national treasure, of which many Americans literally wanted to own a part.

The Star-Spangled Banner's presence in the Smithsonian Institution signifies that it now belongs to all Americans, as does the song it inspired:

'TIS THE STAR-SPANGLED BANNER — O LONG MAY IT WAVE O'ER THE LAND OF THE FREE AND THE HOME OF THE BRAVE!

Appendix 1

The Star-Spangled Banner
By Francis Scott Key

O say can you see, by the dawn's early light,
What so proudly we hail'd at the twilight's last gleaming,
Whose broad stripes and bright stars through the perilous fight
O'er the ramparts we watch'd were so gallantly streaming?
And the rocket's red glare, the bomb bursting in air,
Gave proof through the night that our flag was still there,
O say does that star-spangled banner yet wave
O'er the land of the free and the home of the brave?

On the shore dimly seen through the mists of the deep
Where the foe's haughty host in dread silence reposes,
What is that which the breeze, o'er the towering steep,
As it fitfully blows, half conceals, half discloses?
Now it catches the gleam of the morning's first beam,
In full glory reflected now shines in the stream,
'Tis the star-spangled banner — O long may it wave
O'er the land of the free and the home of the brave!

And where is that band who so vauntingly swore,
That the havoc of war and the battle's confusion
A home and a Country should leave us no more?
Their blood has wash'd out their foul footstep's pollution.
No refuge could save the hireling and slave
From the terror of flight or the gloom of the grave,
And the star-spangled banner in triumph doth wave
O'er the land of the free and the home of the brave.

O thus be it ever when freemen shall stand
Between their lov'd home and the war's desolation!
Blest with vict'ry and peace may the heav'n rescued land
Praise the power that hath made and preserv'd us a nation!
Then conquer we must, when our cause it is just,
And this be our motto — "In God is our trust,"
And the star-spangled banner in triumph shall wave
O'er the land of the free and the home of the brave.

*The spelling and punctuation are from Francis Scott Key's manuscript in the
Maryland Historical Society collection.*

Appendix 2

Lt. Col. George Armistead's Official Report of the Bombardment of Fort McHenry

Fort McHenry, September 24th, 1814

Sir,

A severe indisposition, the effect of great fatigue and exposure, has prevented me heretofore from presenting you with an account of the attack on this post. On the night of Saturday the 10th inst., the British fleet, consisting of ships of the line, frigates, and bomb vessels, amounting in the whole to 30 sail, appeared at the mouth of the river Patapsco, with every indication of an attempt on the city of Baltimore. My own force consisted of one company of United States artillery, under capt. [Frederick] Evans, and two companies of sea fencibles, under captains [M.S.] Bunbury and [William H.] Addison. Of these three companies, 35 men were unfortunately on the sick list, and unfit for duty. I had been furnished with two companies of volunteer artillery from the city of Baltimore, under capt. [John] Berry [Washington Artillerists] and lieut. commandant [Charles] Pennington [Baltimore Independent Artillerists]. To these I must add a very fine company of volunteer artillerists, under judge [Joseph H.] Nicholson [Baltimore Fencibles], who had proffered their services to aid in the defense of this post whenever an attack might be apprehended; also a detachment from commodore [Joshua] Barney's flotilla, under lieutenant [Solomon] Rodman. Brig. general [William] Winder had also furnished me with about six hundred infantry, under the command of lieut. col. [William] Steuart and major [Samuel] Lane, consisting of detachments from the 12th, 14th, 36th, and 38th regiments of United States troops — the total amounting to about 1000 effective men.

On Monday morning very early, it was perceived that the enemy was landing troops on the east side of the Patapsco, distant about ten miles. During that day and the ensuing night, he had brought sixteen ships (including five bomb ships) within about two miles and a half of this Fort. I had arranged my force as follows: the regular artillerists under capt. Evans, and the volunteers under capt. Nicholson, manned the bastions in the Star Fort. Captains Bunbury's, Addison's, Rodman's, Berry's and lieut. commandant Pennington's commands were stationed on the lower works, and the infantry, under lieut. col. Steuart and major Lane, were in the outer ditch, to meet the enemy at his landing, should he attempt one.

On Tuesday morning, about sunrise, the enemy commenced the attack from his five bomb vessels, at the distance of about two miles, when, finding that his shells reached us, he anchored and kept up an incessant and well directed bombardment. We immediately opened our batteries, and kept a brisk fire from our guns and mortars, but unfortunately our shot and shells fell considerably short of him. This was to me a most distressing circumstance; as it left us exposed to a constant and tremendous shower of shells, without the most remote possibility of our doing him the slightest injury. It affords me the highest gratification to state, that although we were left thus exposed, and thus inactive, not a man shrank from the conflict.

About two o'clock P.M. one of the 24 pounders on the south west bastion, under the immediate command of captain Nicholson, was dismounted by a shell, the explosion from which killed his second lieut., and wounded several of his men; the bustle necessarily produced in removing the wounded and replacing the gun, probably induced the enemy to suspect we were in a state of confusion, as he brought in three of his bomb ships, to what I believed to be good striking distance. I immediately ordered a fire to be opened, which was obeyed with alacrity through the whole garrison, and in half an hour those intruders again sheltered themselves by withdrawing beyond our reach. We gave three cheers, and again ceased firing. The enemy continued throwing shells, with one or two slight intermissions, till 1 o'clock on the morning of Wednesday, when it was discovered that he had availed himself of the darkness of the night, and had thrown a considerable force above to our right; they had approached very near to fort Covington, when they began to throw rockets, intended, I presume, to give them an opportunity of examining the shores — as I have since understood, they had detached 1250 picked men, with scaling ladders, for the purpose of storming this fort. We once more had an opportunity of opening our batteries, and kept up a continued blaze for nearly two hours, which had the effect again to drive them off.

In justice to lieut. [Henry] Newcomb, of the U. States navy, who commanded at fort Covington with a detachment of sailors, and lieut. [John A.] Webster, of the flotilla, who commanded the six gun battery near that fort, I ought to state, that during this they kept up an animated, and I believe, a very destructive fire, to which I am persuaded we are much indebted in repulsing the enemy. One of his sunken barges has since been found with two dead men in it; others have been seen floating in the river. The only means we had of directing our guns, was by the blaze of their rockets, and the flashes of their guns. Had they ventured to the same situation in the day time, not a man would have escaped.

The bombardment continued on the part of the enemy until 7 o'clock on Wednesday morning, when it ceased; and about nine, their ships got under weigh, and stood down the river. During the bombardment, which lasted 25 hours (with two short intermissions) from the best calculation I can make, from fifteen to eighteen hundred shells were thrown by the enemy. A few of these fell short. A large proportion burst over us, throwing their fragments among us, and threatening destruction. Many passed over, and about four hundred fell within the works. Two of the public buildings are materially injured, the others but slightly. I am happy to inform you (wonderful as it may appear) that our loss amounts to only four men killed and 24 wounded. The latter will all recover. Among the killed, I have to lament the loss of lieut. [Levi] Claggett, and serjeant [John] Clemm, both of captain Nicholson's volunteers, two men whose fate is to be deplored, not only for their personal bravery, but for their high standing, amiable demeanor, and spotless integrity in private life. Lieut. Russell, of the company under lieut. Pennington, received, early in the attack, a severe contusion in the heel; notwithstanding which he remained at his post during the whole bombardment.

Were I to name individuals who signalised themselves, it would be doing injustice to others. Suffice it to say, that every officer and soldier under my command did their duty to my entire satisfaction.

I have the honour to remain, respectfully, your obedient servant,
G. Armistead, lt. col. U.S. Artillery.

This is the text of Armistead's official report to Secretary of War James Monroe as published in Niles' Weekly Register *on October 1, 1814. The emendations in brackets were supplied by Scott Sheads, Ranger-Historian at Fort McHenry National Monument and Historic Shrine.*

Notes

Introduction

1 "Remarks by the President at National Treasures Tour Kick-Off, National Museum of American History, Washington, D.C., July 13, 1998," Press Release, Office of the White House Press Secretary.

1 The Battle of Baltimore

1 A good account of the battle at North Point is found in Joseph A. Whitehorne, *The Battle for Baltimore* (Baltimore: The Nautical and Aviation Publishing Company of America, 1997), 175–91.

2 For a description of the bombardment based on the most recent evidence, see Anthony S. Pitch, *The Burning of Washington: The British Invasion of 1814* (Annapolis, Md.: Naval Institute Press, 1998), 197–217; also see Scott S. Sheads, *The Rockets' Red Glare: The Maritime Defense of Baltimore in 1814* (Centerville, Md.: Tidewater, 1986). Midshipman Barrett's description of the flag being raised is in Robert J. Barrett, "Naval Recollections of the Late American War," *United Service Journal* (April 1841), 460; Private Munroe's is in Scott S. Sheads, "'Yankee Doodle Played': A Letter from Baltimore, 1814," *Maryland Historical Magazine* 76, no. 4 (winter 1981): 381–82.

3 Virginia Armistead Garber, *The Armistead Family, 1635–1910* (Richmond, Va.: Whittet and Shepperson, 1910), 63; P. W. Filby and Edward G. Howard, *Star-Spangled Books* (Baltimore: Maryland Historical Society, 1972), 23–24.

4 *Niles' Weekly Register,* May 11, 1816;

Margaret Brown Clapthor, "Presentation Pieces in the Museum of History and Technology," in *Contributions from the Museum of History and Technology,* Bulletin 241 (Washington, D.C.: Smithsonian Institution, 1965), 85–86; Eleanore McSherry Fowble, "Rembrandt Peale in Baltimore" (M.A. thesis, University of Delaware, 1965), 98–106; *Niles' Weekly Register,* May 3, 1818; Benson J. Lossing, *The Pictorial Field-Book of the War of 1812* (New York: Harper and Bros., 1868), 960.

2 The Song

1 Ralph J. Robinson, "New Facts in the National Anthem Story," *Baltimore* 49 (September 1956): 33, 35, 37; Filby and Howard, *Star-Spangled Books,* 29–33, 42–45.

2 Henry V.D. Jones (ed.), *Poems of the Late Francis S. Key, Esq.* (New York: Robert Carter and Bros., 1857), 24–25, 26.

3 *Boston Independent Chronicle,* December 30, 1805; *New York Evening Post,* January 9, 1806; *Frederick-Town [Maryland] Herald,* January 18, 1806.

4 William Lichtenwanger, *The Music of the Star-Spangled Banner from Ludgate Hill to Capitol Hill* (Washington, D.C.: Library of Congress, 1977), 4–7, 12, 21–24; Oscar George Theodore Sonneck, *"The Star-Spangled Banner"* (New York: Da Capo Press, 1969), 15–17.

5 George J. Svejda, *History of the Star-Spangled Banner from 1814 to the Present* (Washington, D.C.: U.S. Department of the Interior, 1969), 113–14, 122–24, 130–31; Sonneck, *Star-Spangled Banner,* 84–86; *Baltimore American,* January 13, 1843.

6 Svejda, *History*, 162–219, 222, 232–33, 236, 239–40, 259–60; Sonneck, *Star-Spangled Banner*, 82–83.

7 Svejda, *History*, 329–39.

3 *The Flag*

1 Armistead's letter is quoted in Walter Lord, *By the Dawn's Early Light* (New York: W. W. Norton, 1972), 274. His request for the Fort Niagara flag is described in Brian Leigh Dunnigan, "Fort Niagara's Star-Spangled Banner. A Garrison Color of the War of 1812," *Military Collector and Historian* 50, no. 2 (summer 1998): 75–76.

2 Mary-Paulding Martin, *The Flag House Story* (Baltimore: The Star-Spangled Banner Flag House Association, n.d.), 1–2, 9.

3 Rita Adrosko, "Report on the Star-Spangled Banner Conservation Project, January 26–November 6, 1981," Accession File 54876, National Museum of American History; Amy Venzke and La Tasha Harris to Lonn Taylor, August 9, 1999, Star-Spangled Banner Preservation Project Files, National Museum of American History.

4 Caroline Purdy to Georgiana Armistead Appleton, undated [1876], Appleton Family Papers, Massachusetts Historical Society, Boston.

5 Lord, *Dawn's Early Light*, 365; Mendes I. Cohen to George Preble, August 24, 1873, Preble Papers; "The Star-Spangled Banner," *The American Historical Record* 2, no. 3 (January 1873), 24.

6 The changes in the flag's design and the origin of the Betsy Ross story are described in William Rea Furlong and Byron McCandless, *So Proudly We Hail: The History of the United States Flag* (Washington, D.C.: Smithsonian Institution Press, 1981), 98–101, 115–19, 158. The symbolism of the flag's colors is discussed in Whitney Smith, *The Flag Book of the United States* (New York: William Morrow and Co., Inc., 1975), 87.

4 *An Armistead Family Treasure*

1 Georgiana Appleton to George Preble, July 5, 1873. George Henry Preble Papers, American Antiquarian Society, Worcester, Mass.; *New York Herald*, August 4, 1895; *Baltimore Sun*, June 14, 1907; *Boston Herald*, August 31, 1889; *Annual Report of the Board of Regents of the Smithsonian Institution, 1907* (Washington, D.C.: Government Printing Office, 1909), 39.

2 The Civil and Military Arrangements for the Reception of Major General La Fayette in the City of Baltimore, Francis Scott Key Papers, Maryland Historical Society, Baltimore, Md.; *Baltimore American*, October 9, 1824; *Baltimore Sunday News*, September 8, 1889; *Baltimore American*, August 29, 1889; *Baltimore American*, July 4, 1834; *Baltimore American*, September 14, 1839.

3 Edward S. Delaplaine, *Francis Scott Key* (New York: Biography Press, 1937), 477–78; *Baltimore Sun*, January 13, 1843; *Baltimore Sun*, January 14, 1843; Young Men's Whig National Convention of Ratification Held in Baltimore City on the Second of May, 1844 (n.p., n.d.), 2, National Museum of American History, Political History Collection, Becker 227739, 1844, A24.

4 Interview, Lonn Taylor with Pattie Cook, Louisa, Virginia, July 12, 1997.

5 Appleton to Preble, July 5, 1873, Preble Papers; Preble to Appleton, June 30, 1873, Appleton Papers; *Baltimore Sun*, October 13, 1873; Baltimore City Register of Wills, Vol. 30: 166–70.

6 Appleton to Appleton, December 30, 1861, Appleton Papers; Garber, *The Armistead Family*, 71–72; *Baltimore Sun*, September 9, 1861.

7 *New York Herald*, August 4, 1895.

8 Georgiana Appleton to George Preble, June 17, 1873, Preble Papers.

9 *The American Historical Record* 2, no. 13 (January 1873): 24.

10 Appleton to Preble, February 18, 1873, Preble Papers.

11 Preble to Appleton, February 26, 1873, March 13, 1873, Appleton Papers; Appleton to Preble, March 8, 1873, Preble Papers; Preble to Appleton, June 22, 1873, Appleton Papers; George H. Preble, *Three Historic Flags and Three September Victories* (Boston: n.p., 1873), 21–22.

12 Preble to Appleton, August 21, 1873; December 1, 1874; James Lick to Appleton, January 4, 1874; Stephen Salisbury to Appleton, June 3, 1874; Appleton Papers; Stephen Salisbury to Preble, September 14, 1873, Preble Papers.

13 Charles B. Norton to Appleton, March 27, 1873; Alice Etting to Appleton, December 29, 1873; Appleton to Etting (draft), January 18, 1874; Preble to Appleton, October 6, 1875, Appleton Papers.

14 Preble to Appleton, July 27, 1876; August 14, 1876, Appleton Papers;

Appleton to Preble, September 9, 1876, Preble Papers.

15 Appleton to Appleton, November 2, 1875, Appleton Papers.

16 Nathan Appleton, *The Star Spangled Banner* (Boston: Lockwood, Brooks, and Co., 1877), 3–4, 33–34; *New York Herald*, June 16, 1877.

17 Appleton to Preble, July 5, 1873; Appleton to Preble, July 16, 1873; April 27, 1876; Preble Papers; Georgiana Appleton to Nathan Appleton, April 15, 1861; William Stuart Appleton to Nathan Appleton, April 6, 1861; Georgiana Appleton to Eben Appleton, October 8, 1865; Appleton Papers; Mary Howard to Alice Etting, December 13, 1873, Frank Etting Papers, Historical Society of Pennsylvania, Philadelphia.

18 Eben Appleton to Preble, March 15, 1879, Preble Papers; *Baltimore American*, September 2, 1889; *Baltimore American*, September 3, 1889; *Baltimore Sun*, October 14, 1880; *Baltimore American*, November 30, 1883.

19 *Baltimore American*, August 29, 1889; *Baltimore American*, September 3, 1889; *Baltimore American*, September 8, 1889; *New York Mail and Express*, August 30, 1889; *New York Sun*, April 7, 1907.

5 *The Star-Spangled Banner and the Smithsonian Institution*

1 *Baltimore Sun,* June 30, 1907; *Baltimore American*, July 10, 1907; Baylor to Walcott, May 29, 1907; Appleton to Baylor, May 24, 1907; Walcott to Baylor, June 4, 1907; Appleton to Walcott, June 11, 1907; Appleton to Walcott, June 25, 1907; Rathbun to Appleton, July 8,

1907; Rathbun to Appleton, July 11, 1907, Accession File 54876, National Museum of American History, Washington, D.C.

2 Walcott to Rathbun, December 19, 1913; Rathbun to Walcott, December 22, 1913; Walcott to Bibbins, December 29, 1913; Appleton to Walcott, January 5, 1914; Walcott to Appleton, January 8, 1914; Appleton to Walcott, January 10, 1914; Accession File.

3 Bibbins to Walcott, January 26, 1914; Bibbins to Walcott, June 27, 1914; Bibbins to Walcott, July 1, 1914; Appleton to Walcott, August 31, 1914; Accession File; *National Star-Spangled Banner Centennial, Baltimore, Maryland, September 6 to 13, 1914* (Baltimore: National Star-Spangled Banner Centennial Commission, 1914), 111.

4 Appleton to Preble, March 8, 1873, Preble Papers.

5 Belote to J. E. Holmes, February 3, 1914, Accession File.

6 Holmes to Rathbun, February 10, 1914; Isabel Rives to William Ravenel, March 10, 1914; Rathbun to Fowler, March 25, 1914.

7 Belote to Holmes, February 3, 1914, Accession File; Sue Lenthe, "Don't Give Up the Flags: The Preservation Efforts of Amelia Bold Fowler and Katherine Fowler Richey," *Piecework* 3, no. 4 (July/August 1995): 60–64; U.S. Patent No. 1,075,206, issued October 7, 1913.

8 Mary E. Ludenig, "Saving the Star-Spangled Banner," *St. Nicholas Magazine* 59, no. 9 (July 1932): 464; Samuel Davis to William Ravenel, April 10, 1914; William Ravenel to Amelia Fowler,

May 6, 1914; Theodore Belote to J. E. Graf, January 18, 1940; Accession File.

9 Belote to Graf, May 4, 1938, Accession File; *Annual Report of the Board of Regents of the Smithsonian Institution, 1945* (Washington, D.C.: Government Printing Office, 1946), 10.

10 Edgar M. Howell to Frank Taylor, August 16, 1961, Accession File; William E. Boyle to Howell, November 29, 1963, Folder 13, Star-Spangled Banner File, Textile Collection, National Museum of American History; Interview, Lonn Taylor with Donald Kloster, August 16, 1999.

11 Rita J. Adrosko, "Report on the Star-Spangled Banner Conservation Project, December 9, 1981," Accession File; Paul R. Jett, "The Cleaning and Examination of the Star-Spangled Banner: A Report Submitted to the Division of Conservation, September 29, 1982," Accession File.

12 "Smithsonian's Star-Spangled Banner Conservation Laboratory and Exhibition Open at National Museum of American History," Press Release, updated August 2, 1999, Office of Public Affairs, National Museum of American History.

Bibliography

Unpublished Sources

Baltimore. City Register of Wills.

Baltimore. Maryland Historical Society. Francis Scott Key Papers.

Boston. Massachusetts Historical Society. Appleton Family Papers.

Fowble, Eleanore McSherry, "Rembrandt Peale in Baltimore." M.A. thesis, University of Delaware, 1965.

Washington, D.C. National Museum of American History. Accession Files, Textile Collection Files, Star-Spangled Banner Preservation Project Files.

Worcester, Mass. American Antiquarian Society. George Henry Preble Papers.

Newspapers

Baltimore American, 1807, 1824, 1834, 1839, 1843, 1883, 1889.

Baltimore Sun, 1843, 1873, 1880, 1907.

Baltimore Sunday News, 1889.

Boston Herald, 1889.

Boston Independent Chronicle, 1805.

Frederick-Town [Maryland] Herald, 1806.

New York Evening Post, 1806.

New York Herald, 1877, 1895.

New York Mail and Express, 1889.

New York Sun, 1907.

Niles' Weekly Register, 1814, 1816, 1818.

Richmond Daily Whig, 1841.

Books and Articles

Annual Report of the Board of Regents of the Smithsonian Institution, 1907. Washington, D.C.: Government Printing Office, 1909.

Annual Report of the Board of Regents of the Smithsonian Institution, 1945. Washington, D.C.: Government Printing Office, 1946.

Appleton, Nathan, *The Star-Spangled Banner.* Boston: Lockwood, Brooks, and Co., 1877.

Barrett, Robert J., "Naval Recollections of the Late American War," *United Service Journal* (April 1841): 455–67.

Clapthor, Margaret Brown, "Presentation Pieces in the Museum of History and Technology." In *Contributions from the Museum of History and Technology, Bulletin 241.* Washington, D.C.: Smithsonian Institution Press, 1965.

Delaplaine, Edward S., *Francis Scott Key.* New York: Biography Press, 1937.

Dunnigan, Brian Leigh, "Fort Niagara's Star-Spangled Banner: A Garrison Color of the War of 1812," *Military Collector and Historian* 50: 74–79.

Filby, P. W., and Howard, Edward G., *Star-Spangled Books.* Baltimore: Maryland Historical Society, 1972.

Furlong, William Rea, and McCandless, Byron, *So Proudly We Hail: The History of the United States Flag.* Washington, D.C.: Smithsonian Institution Press, 1981.

Garber, Virginia Armistead, *The Armistead Family, 1635–1910.* Richmond: Whittet and Shepperson, 1910.

Guenter, Scot M., *The American Flag, 1777–1924: Cultural Shifts from Creation to Codification.* Rutherford, N.J: Fairleigh Dickinson University Press, 1990.

Jones, Henry V. D. (ed.), *Poems of the Late Francis S. Key, Esq.* New York: Robert Carter and Bros., 1857.

Lenthe, Sue, "Don't Give Up the Flags: The Preservation Efforts of Amelia Bold Fowler and Katherine Fowler Richey," *Piecework* 3 (July/August 1995): 60–65.

Lichtenwanger, William, *The Music of the Star-Spangled Banner from Ludgate Hill to Capitol Hill*. Washington, D.C.: Library of Congress, 1977.

Lord, Walter, *By the Dawn's Early Light*. New York: W. W. Norton, 1972.

Lossing, Benson J., *The Pictorial Field-Book of the War of 1812*. New York: Harper and Brothers, 1868.

———, "The Star-Spangled Banner," *The American Historical Record* 2 (January 1873): 24.

Ludenig, Mary E., "Saving the Star-Spangled Banner," *St. Nicholas Magazine* 59: 462–465.

Martin, Mary-Paulding, *The Flag House Story*. Baltimore: The Star-Spangled Banner Flag House Association, n.d.

National Star-Spangled Banner Centennial, Baltimore, Maryland, September 6 to 13, 1914. Baltimore: National Star-Spangled Banner Centennial Commission, 1914.

Pitch, Anthony S., *The Burning of Washington: The British Invasion of 1814*. Annapolis, Md.: Naval Institute Press, 1998.

Preble, George H., *Three Historic Flags and Three September Victories*. Boston: n.p., 1873.

Robinson, Ralph J., "New Facts in the National Anthem Story," *Baltimore* 49 (September, 1956): 32–37.

Sheads, Scott, "'Yankee Doodle Played': A Letter from Baltimore, 1814," *Maryland Historical Magazine* 76: 380–82.

———, *The Rockets' Red Glare: The Maritime Defense of Baltimore in 1814*. Centerville, Md.: Tidewater, 1986.

Smith, Whitney, *The Flag Book of the United States*. New York: William Morrow and Co., Inc., 1975.

Sonneck, Oscar George Theodore, *Report on "The Star-Spangled Banner," "Hail Columbia," "America," and "Yankee Doodle,"* New York: Da Capo Press, 1969.

Svejda, George J., *History of the Star-Spangled Banner from 1814 to the Present*. Washington, D.C.: U.S. Department of the Interior, 1969.

Watts, Steven, *The Republic Reborn*. Baltimore: The Johns Hopkins University Press, 1987.

Whitehorne, Joseph A., *The Battle for Baltimore*. Baltimore: The Nautical and Aviation Publishing Company of America, 1997.

Acknowledgments

First I would like to thank The Pew Charitable Trusts for its catalytic role in committing the initial support for the Star-Spangled Banner Preservation Project, of which this book is a part. The Trusts' significant leadership stimulated funding from the United States Congress and The John S. and James L. Knight Foundation. Its partnership with First Lady Hillary Rodham Clinton and The White House Millennium Council led to the project's major support being provided by Polo Ralph Lauren. Mr. Lauren's generosity extended beyond the Preservation Project; it included his support for a national advertising campaign in association with Save America's Treasures at the National Trust for Historic Preservation. The National Museum of American History at the Smithsonian Institution is grateful to all for their extraordinary leadership in preserving the Star-Spangled Banner.

The first three chapters of this book bring together in one place the scholarship of authors who over the past ninety years have probed the story of the flag and the anthem in publications ranging from government reports to books written for popular audiences. My debts to these authors are acknowledged, at least in part, in the endnotes and in the bibliography. The last two chapters present previously unpublished material that is largely the result of research in the George Henry Preble Papers at the American Antiquarian Society in Worcester, Massachusetts; the Appleton Family Papers at the Massachusetts Historical Society in Boston; the Enoch Pratt Free Library and the Maryland Historical Society in Baltimore, Maryland; and the archives of the Smithsonian Institution.

For guidance and assistance in conducting this research, I would first like to thank Scott Sheads and Anna von Lunz of the Fort McHenry National Monument and Historic Site. They have been valued collaborators from the very beginning of this project. Sally Johnston and Pat

Pilling of the Star-Spangled Banner Flag House and 1812 Museum, Joan B. Chaison and Thomas Knoles of the American Antiquarian Society, Peter Drummey of the Massachusetts Historical Society, and Pamela Henson of the Smithsonian Institution Archives have also rendered invaluable assistance.

At the National Museum of American History, Ron Becker, Lonnie Bunch, Jim Gardner, Paula Johnson, Donald Kloster, Susan Myers, Suzanne Thomassen-Krauss, and Marilyn Zoidis have been sympathetic listeners and thoughtful critics. Rita Adrosko, Doris Bowman, Kathy Dirks, Amy Venzke, and La Tasha Harris have provided valuable information. Interns Susan Clark and Sascha Scott provided research assistance and helped to solve several historical puzzles. Martha Davidson has tracked down elusive photographs and obtained permission for their use in this book. Carol Frost has gone far beyond the usual call of duty in coordinating the various aspects of this entire project.

I especially would like to thank the members of the Armistead family who have shared information and memories with me, including George Armistead III, Henry Armistead, Robert Bradford, Tom and Beverly Gordon, Christopher Morton, Edwin Morton, and Theodore Morton.

Finally I would like to thank my editors, Diana Cohen Altman at the Smithsonian Institution and Nicole Columbus at Harry N. Abrams, Inc., for their painstaking care, which has made the text both readable and accurate.

Lonn Taylor
Historian, Division of Social History
National Museum of American History
Smithsonian Institution